The Shout

The Shout

When I didn't want to listen,
The "shout" gave meaning to my life.

Beverly Ruiz

Copyright © 2020 by Beverly Ruiz.

Library of Congress Control Number:		2020914538
ISBN:	Hardcover	978-1-5065-3355-1
	Softcover	978-1-5065-3354-4
	eBook	978-1-5065-3353-7

Print information available on the last page.

Rev. date: 28/08/2020

To order additional copies of this book, contact:
Palibrio
1663 Liberty Drive
Suite 200
Bloomington, IN 47403
Toll Free from the U.S.A 877.407.5847
Toll Free from Mexico 01.800.288.2243
Toll Free from Spain 900.866.949
From other International locations +1.812.671.9757
Fax: 01.812.355.1576
orders@palibrio.com
814628

CONTENTS

How much
I miss them...

As a father has compassion
on his children,
so the Lord has compassion
on those who fear Him.
Psalm 103:13

*To my parents
with love!*
– Beverly Ruiz –

DEDICATION

I DEDICATE THIS book first to You, my God, you are my inspiration; without You, my story would not exist. Thanks for the times You spoke to me and "shouted" at me, you brought out the best in me, and I know that you are still working.

To my parents, who, with their immense love, gave everything to get me ahead and have been the protagonists of my life.

To my children, Jonathan, Beverly Ann, and Josué, who are my inspiration, motivation, and reason to continue fighting. To the children that God brought me together with the love of my life, Ariadnie, Lizmary, Isaac, and Rafael, I love them. To my daughters-in-law Karla and Sarah, who came to my life to fill it with love. To Juan, Evelyn, and Jose Negron for loving and caring for my treasures.

To my grandchildren Kiara, Yadiel, Valeria, Juan Carlos, Arianna, and Julius Eli, you are my gift from God, and this is the legacy that I, your grandmother has left you.

To my sister Marlene and her husband Victor, to my brother Javier and his wife Mycheri to my nephews Giselle, Pedro, Giraliz, Christian, and Jadeli; thanks for much love.

To my friends and sisters, Olga, Sheila, and Isabel, thank you for being part of my life.

To all the angels that God put in my way; Joivan & Luciane Jiménez, Letty Resto, Gloria Zapata, Joany E. Meyers, Keila Carrillo, Damaris Torres, Nilsa I. Colon, Freddie Méndez, Norma Valcárcel, Lymari Martínez, Raúl López, Rafael Pena, Glenda Solís, Julio Valentín, Marilú González, Myrna Rosado, Vercelly López, Ramses & Analys, Jorge, Nilsa & Karla Santana.

To Mary Jones, Elaine Williams, Retania Patterson, Grace Swiontek & Donald Manning, thank you for all the love and support, this book is for all of you.

To all of those who have influenced my spiritual life and have been my teachers in the word of God and to every person who has remained by my side supporting and loving me unconditionally, there are no words that express my gratitude.

To Omalier Ruiz, who was not part of the story that was originally written, but since he came into my life, he motivated me to do this version in English. He knew that behind this beautiful project was a majestic plan from the creator. Thank you infinitely, for being my inspiration and my teacher in the faith and helping me develop this new project of love. I love you!

Thank you all for being a part of my life and determining to love me and stay by my side and accept me with my defects and virtues, this book is for all of you.

ACKNOWLEDGMENT

I WOULD HAVE TO write a whole book to thank every person and angel that God has put to help me make my way in life. I will only mention those who strictly believed in my book and helped me make it a reality. Also, I include those who have worked on the English version.

Spanish version:
Firstly, to **Sheila Birriel**, thank you for helping me understand God's message. Your insistence that I write a book was key to making it happen at the moment God determined.

Carlos Tarrats, thank you for listening and supporting me and, above all, for giving me the tool to start working on my dream.

To my friend *Evelyn Santiago*, for many years, you have been by my side supporting me, this time it was no different. At the time I called you, you did not hesitate to answer. Thanks to you, this book has been written with clarity and professionalism.

To my sister **Estelina Burgos**, when God crossed our paths again, I asked you for help, and without thinking, you edited and took care of the last details of this project, making you part of my dream.

To my friend *Jonathan Soto*, for your support, professionalism, and sensitivity.

To my sister and brother, **Marlene** and **Javier** and my sister-in-law **Mycheri**, who lovingly adopted my dream as if it were yours, helping me define it and present it with commitment and professionalism.

To my brother **Josean Espinosa**, cover photographer. Thank you for your unconditional support and for those images that reflect the sacred intention of this love project.

To my friend, **Luis Santos**, for your support and professionalism.

To my friend **Gregory González**, thank you for interpreting the image that God gave me in dreams and making them come true by showing them on the cover.

English Version:

Seven years later, God integrates key people into this new project who has made it possible for this version to carry the full message with the same love and passion written in the original version.

To my daughter-in-law **Karla Franco**, who adopted this project as if it were her own, doing the full translation of this book. Thank you for so much love, I know that God has great rewards for your life. I love you!

To **Solimar García Hance**, for your editing work. Thank you for agreeing to be part of this project that will transform lives, and you will be part of it.

To **Pedro Alexis Guadalupe**, graphic artist and my nephew, who transformed the original cover into the English version. For your unconditional love and support.

To my sister **Marlene Ruiz**, a graphic artist who works the entire promotion and is always by my side, supporting me in each of my projects.

To **Wilfred J. Lugo**, for always being by our side. For helping us in the media campaign and helping us spread the love of Jesus.

To **Omalier Ruiz** for being my ideal help and working so that this book reaches every corner of the world. For loving God above all things. For loving me unconditionally and making me so happy.

Thank you to everyone who has been a part of my life and this story. To those who remain and to those who are no longer with us, without you, I could not have reached the final goal.

To you, my **God**, because you are the reason for my existence and the purpose of my life, infinite thanks.

THANKS TO EVERYONE!

PROLOGUE

THE FIRST TIME I met Beverly, I was impacted by her love and her affection. It seemed as if we knew each other for many years. Seeing her smile and her passion I never imagined she had a story and such a powerful trajectory.

I comprehended that the size of her heart is the result of years of trials, pain and victory. The Shout will touch your heart and will give you strength to keep on walking. If this short woman was able to make it, you also can.

Pastor Joivan Jiménez
Actor/Worshiper/ Life Coach

INTRODUCTION

WHAT IS A shout? It is a change of tone of voice higher than normal demanding immediate attention, besides being a spontaneous form of expression to any emotion; be it fright, botheration, joy, surprise, but above all of PRECAUTION.

If we want to give a surprise, we shout; if we want to cheer our players on our team, we shout. We shout when it is necessary to prevent or avoid a situation, mishap or accident; but we also shout when we need help or feel pain. One shout can avoid situations, but it can also mark us for life.

The shout has no gender, no religion, no race; it does not belong to any government. It neither belongs to any social group, the rich shouts the same as the poor. The shout has no age; the elders, the adults, the youth, the children, and the baby shout. The shout is a resource that we must accentuate our emotions and express them with the certainty that we will be heard.

As I was thinking of a title for my book, praying before going to sleep I said: "Lord, give me the title, one that is short, precise and overall, that catches attention." When I woke up, that was the word I had in my mind; "The Shout."

That is precisely what you will receive through this book. There will be many "Shouts" that will bring you to a stop and obligate you to pay attention and better analyze your decisions.

Throughout this lecture, you will learn to identify the different "Shouts" that God gives you to take you along the path you need to walk and thus get to where you will feel fulfilled; where you will enjoy the inner peace during the hard moments you may be going through. In no way, "The Shout" promotes violence or verbal mistreat; it is just a metaphoric term I will use to get your attention according to the needs, situations, and circumstances that you may be going through.

The main idea of this book is to show you that God created you with a purpose, that you were not an accident. He made you a dreamer and gave you the tools to fight and achieve your dreams. He wants man to experiment the sensation, pleasure, and pride that is felt when we see our dreams come true. He wants man to feel what He felt when He turned His dreams into a reality; when He looked at His creation, and when He looked at you.

This shout is a cry for help in your life; stop, and reconsider! Start working on your dreams, discover how wonderful you are. Dare yourself to win at life; if I did it, you can too!

I've been thinking about my dreams for years. As time went by, I kept changing ideas and flowing with the circumstances, which would make me change my dreams afterward. After each experience, I would ask myself, "What do I want from life? What does life want from me?".

After spending years of looking at how to survive each" problem" (at least that is how I called it at that time), I understood that all those "problems" were necessary to become the human being and woman I am today. The "shouting" life had showed me the path I had to take.

If you are going through difficult moments, if you have not yet defined what your purpose in life is, if you think your problems are the greatest that exist, if you can't find the way to victory, if you don't believe you have the courage, if you don't know how to manage love, if you don't know how to reach your dreams, then this book is for you.

If you don't identify with any of the previous situations, you are a privileged person and with this book you will learn to have a grateful heart and willing to listen.

I am an ordinary person, who thousands of times, asked myself the same questions as you. There were times where I was not capable of dreaming, I thought I was something small that didn't deserve to exist. I don't know what your experiences might be, but through this book I will share mine, which trained and motivated me to share them with you; and desperately and in "shouts", tell you that everything has a purpose and a solution.

Through real-life stories, illustrations, metaphors, and humor, I will take you to discover that you are a masterpiece and that you are of incalculable value.

You will also get to know the power of gratitude and the treasure of having a humble and simple heart. You will understand that if this was the last day you have to live, until today it was worth it to fight for your dreams.

CHAPTER 1

When we don't have options

I DON'T EXACTLY remember when the desire to write a book started. I think since I was very little, I would hear my dad mention that was his dream. One way or another, it was something that I began to visualize and converted that idea into my goal as well.

Whenever I felt the need to start working on the book, I would ask myself the same questions: "What will the theme be? Who is going to be interested in what I write? How extraordinary can my life be to be embodied in a book?

I spent years meditating on this; many times, not to say daily, I would find myself writing in my mind everything that would happen to me. I imagined how I would write it and would close that thought with a teaching. Other times, I would write notes that I saved for many years, and now I can share them with you.

After my best friends' insistence, especially Sheila, and going through many situations, I understood that this voice that I felt within for many years was shouting what I had to do, placing in my hands the way to make it happen and make it a reality. It gave me the perfect tool: MY OWN LIFE.

You may have asked yourself many times: Why were you born? Why do you have the parents you have or had? Why are things not the way you desire? Why were you mistreated or abused? Why do you lack the courage to control your desires knowing they are not correct? Why do you lack the courage to make decisions?

On the other hand, I've met people that have everything, and have also asked themselves many questions: Why do I have everything? Why does nothing excite me? Why don't I have real friends? I don't know with whom of these people you identify yourself with, but just like you, I have also asked myself thousands of these and other questions. I felt frustrated because my life was not what I desired.

As years passed, those questions started to diminish; I'm still unclear if it is because I have the answers or simply because I am not interested in knowing anymore.

We all know that we must go through different stages, that are supposed to have a chronological order. When we are kids, our parents or the people that raised us are responsible for making our decisions. These facts expose us to see that if our parents or the people that raised us are not emotionally balanced, our foundations will not be firm and let alone our emotional development.

In this first stage, we don't have an option to decide which parents we want or in which country or place we want to be born; we can even choose the social level we want to live in. When I started to grow up and was quite clear of the difference between good and evil, I began to compare. It bothered me, and I couldn't understand why I was not given the option to decide how I wanted to live my own life.

I come from a middle-class family. We never lacked food, we had no luxuries, and my parents made sure that we never lacked the basic needs to live. My family was composed of my parents, one sister, my younger brother and me (the oldest sister). It was a confusing childhood, two parents with a twenty-year age difference, two religions, and two completely different characters. A divorce, that from my part, differently than most children, I desperately desired.

In those times, I just hoped to sleep in peace and in my own bed, not at my neighbors, where many times my siblings and I ended up after my parents fought; these fights sometimes got out of control. I didn't want to hear those "shouts" that would make us run out of fear and confusion.

It was in this stage of my life where the questions started. I envied my friends who had families that could go out to a park or a beach together, without ending everything in a war. The difference in age and character of my parents created a distance between them and us. It seemed as if no one noticed how the situation was marking my life and my siblings.

"The Shout." When God put that title in my mind, I quickly did a walkthrough of my life; within seconds, I realized that the "shouts" had always been part of me. These are the "shouts" that mark us negatively; they are the ones that, despite the time, are still present in our memories.

I do not mean by this that in my family, there were no moments that we can remember with joy and gratitude. Our mother was always a very organized and elegant woman. According to her, she had a tough childhood and suffered mistreatments that, until this day, she hasn't been able to forget or overcome.

For many years she lived with spiritual and mental conflicts that kept her in depression most of the time. Even so, she always worked untiringly as a stylist for over forty years. At that time, one of the best in our area. She always worked hard to supply for us and give us all the things we needed. She was and still is, a person of strong character, but also very sensible and capable of risking everything to defend the weak.

My mother made decisions out of impulse in a desperate search to find love and that other half that completed her. According to her, her marriage with my father was an impulse, a desperate exit, or revenge. I will never have that cleared up, but it was evident that it was not out of love.

After the divorce, my mother tried vainly to find that man that could make her happy. In some way, those attempts were affecting our lives and provoking us to see relationships with distrust and instability. Each one of my mom's separations costs us all; we had to suffer her depression without detailing how much each relationship's abrupt end affected us.

My father, twenty years older than my mother, Christian, elegant, one of the most intellectual men that I have ever met, with only a third-grade education, could prepare the university thesis of many students. He was also a poetry writer and prepared investigation studies. He spoke various languages, and his passion was History. He was an amateur in the Bible, the History of the United States, Puerto Rico, and Europe. He would memorize events with names and dates. I inherited from him the passion for writing, but never History. As a fun fact, I remember the times that I would make him change the color of his face, annoyed because after telling me the History of the French Revolution, he would ask me questions about it, and the only thing I could remember was that it was about France.

My father, as I was able to describe, had many talents and abilities. He was a man of faith and completely committed to God. However, when I try to remember a conversation with him, that was not about religion, history, mathematics, or if I tried to describe his dreams or frustrations, I realize that I don't have a clear memory. We never really got to know him. Occasionally he mentioned, "his dream to write a book."

Trying to find information to write, I asked my younger brother: "What can you tell me about dad?" After a long silence, he said: "I don't know, I never got to know him." Obviously, the age difference between father and son was clear; to my brother this meant having a dad going to his sixties, tired, and with a totally different mentality than his.

I think like my brother, my dad lived locked inside himself; he was conformed with his knowledge and never took advantage of them. He was not interested in getting to another level on this earth. He always emphasized that his richness was not this world, but in the "Celestial Mansions."

His long hours of silence would make him feel absent among us. On the other hand, he was humble and helpful, spending the entire year collecting used toys to fix them and take them to orphanages on Christmas. Since he was at an advanced age, he couldn't see very well, and I remember that many times my sister and I would receive dolls with white bodies and brown heads. Funny! But regardless, we were always grateful for our gifts.

I also remember that in the afternoon, he would go to the neighbors' houses to collect the leftover food they had to give to the dogs that lived in the street. I have many anecdotes and teachings from my father that I will share with you throughout this book.

My father died at the age of seventy-four. His departure still hurts us, but the most ironic of all this is that after his death and collecting all his writings and poetry, it was when we really learned how much he loved us and what he thought of us. He was shy to express emotions, and it was not until that moment that we really got to know him.

We should not judge our parents; mine were each their own way, the best they could; separated, they were friends; together, they were a time bomb.

I have only walked you briefly through our childhood, so you can see how our parents' decisions and attitudes affect us, or of those people designated by God to build the foundation of what our lives will be.

I know of people that even when they are in full maturity, their childhood continues to affect them and that the first stage of their lives keeps marking every emotion, determining their present and generally, if we are talking about a difficult childhood, destroying their future.

My mom was a key point in my life. She came from a tough childhood. She suffered the poverty of her time; her mother was a very strict and hard person due to the experiences she suffered. Besides, her older sister was a victim of mental illness at the age of twelve. Her father was a cobbler, a man well-loved by everyone, and had a good sense of humor. I remember his jokes and games that would make us laugh. My grandmother had control of the house; my grandfather preferred not to contradict her. These were some of the things that our mom told us that, in a way, justify the way she managed her own life.

At that time, the only law our grandparents knew was: "a clean stick and hard hand, so they get shame". They would call that "discipline". Not that it was all wrong; the discipline was necessary, but not to exaggerate, capable of damaging and causing trauma for the rest of that child's life. We knew that our mother had been hurt, but it wasn't until years passed that we realized how significant and disastrous the damage was and how much influence it had on her.

Our grandparents had also suffered a lot of mistreating, besides experiencing the madness of their oldest daughter; they also did the best they could with the education they already had. I could not judge them either. I would have loved to know them better.

When we are kids, we don't have the option to choose, we are only spectators, and as if we were a bank, life keeps depositing emotions and feelings that, with time, we will withdraw. In my case, the instability of our parents, the lack of communication, puberty, and all the hormonal changes that this entails, led me to early maturity.

While my dad spread awareness in us through religion, my mom, with the best intention, did the same, but with the resources and understanding that she had at the time. Although she did not comprehend at the time, she was not defined spiritually; she said to be catholic but did not visit church frequently. Furthermore, she combined it with some spiritism and was very devoted to her saints.

She had an Indian whom she smoked tobacco and would put fruits, a Buddha she would rub the belly and ask for wishes, a baby Jesus to whom she would pray her rosaries, a virgin, and other saints like Saint Lazarus and Saint Martin de Porres. There also had to be elephants with their back facing the door for "good luck". She was writing for years about what a spiritual voice would dictate her, and we got used to seeing notebooks utterly full of her writings.

Many times, out of curiosity, I would secretly read what she wrote, and it was always a conversation between my mom and a mysterious entity. She would tell it things, and that entity would answer. Lastly, if memory serves, the "OUIJA" was what completed this cycle, leaving her mentally and emotionally destroyed.

We lived with our mom, and unfortunately, we had to be part of this confusing spiritual cycle. Me being the oldest of my siblings, I was more aware of what was going on. In her desperate search to get rid of that voice that was driving her crazy, she decided to visit this house that was very close from where we lived and where spiritual rituals were practiced.

She searched for all the help she could; visited psychiatrists, psychologists, doctors, priests, anyway; tried everything without success. She could not sleep, have fun and even when she was working, at times, ran away like a "robot", looking for a paper to write everything that voice was telling her.

I have never been able to forget that place, I remember each ritual that was practiced. The most impressive part was to see how the "mediums" would go in a "trance" and start to speak in different voices and tongues that I could not understand. I was impressed to see how they would shake and hit over a table. There were glass containers with water, tobacco, necklaces, images of Indians to which they laid money and fruits, and ointments that they rubbed on their bodies. The smell of incense was strong and intense.

Although I did not understand it then, now I know that this experience was only preparing me for the purpose that I already had in life. It was at this stage where I inexplicably lived the experience that marked my life and many other people's lives.

To do this story, I had to stop writing for a few weeks and try to remember names. I started to make phone calls and send emails to people who were witnesses, being present during that experience, in order to collect the correct information, organize my memories and be able to share it truthfully.

Many answered my phone call and messages, and like expressed, despite all the pain that caused them to go back to that stage of their lives, they agreed to do it because, like me, they also needed closure for that experience. It was harder for them since they watched and listened; while I only have vague memories of what happened.

We were between the ages of twelve and fourteen. When we are children, we have a very abstract idea of what is real or fantasy. We don't know how to clearly distinguish between good or bad and it is very easy for our feelings, emotions, and thoughts to be manipulated or altered. We don't have the maturity, control, or authority over our lives. We do not have options, and we are defenseless facing the decisions from our parents or the people responsible for us.

The experience that I will tell in this next chapter will show you how vulnerable we are as kids. It took me many years to understand it, but I realized that we all must go through sad situations and live difficult moments. There will always be someone with harder experiences than others. Comparing ourselves or questioning God will never lead us to understand the reasons.

God does not expect you to understand him, but to believe him, no matter your circumstances. The moment will come that you will be able to understand the motives and reasons; then, you will be able to decide and choose what you want for your life. In my case, despite being a girl, the circumstances obligated me to choose between heaven and hell.

CHAPTER 2

Between heaven and hell

I N 1975, AFTER my parents' divorce, my days elapsed between church, school, and the visit from time to time to that house that I remember with horror.

As I mentioned, not everything was bad or difficult at the time, my mom was a happy woman, and there were times we shared and laughed at her stories and jokes. On the other side, my dad made sure to pick us up every Saturday to take us to church. Then, at night, we would end up in church activities, games, music and laughter. That was the way we had fun at that time.

The academy where we studied was christian and taught us the doctrines of my dad's religion. I remember, arriving at the academy was the most wonderful feeling and experience that I could live back then. Meeting with my friends filled me with the energy to face what, on the other hand, would steal my peace.

At that time, I cultivated two of the four people that today, (38) years later, can say that are one of the "treasures of my life"; my friends and sisters. Those who have always, even in the worst moments of that time and to this day, been by my side: Olga and Sheila.

I was always spontaneous, impulsive, accelerated, romantic, always in love, stubborn, cunning, and above all, very flirtatious and vain. I needed everyone's attention. Let me give you an example; I remember that we lived in a commercial area. That being said, our house was surrounded by businesses and the street in front of my house was very crowded with cars and people. When I had an activity or simply was going out, I would get dressed and stand in front of the house where all the cars passed. If NOBODY SHOUTED A COMPLIMENT or honked at me, I would go back in, change clothes, and go back out as many times necessary until someone noticed me. With this, I accomplished two things; making sure I looked good and captured everyone's attention.

I always felt a disadvantage among my peers. The emotional instability had provoked a lot of insecurity. Somehow, I was looking to fill that need of feeling cared for and protected.

My parents always worked to supply our basic needs, especially our mother, who always fought to get us ahead, but they did not realize that there were other things we needed that were essential and necessary for our development. They did not visit the school or participated in activities like other parents did. Their unawareness brought them to neglect areas that were extremely important to us.

I loved to sing (it was my passion), something that I did with my brother and sister since I was little. When we sang together, my parents were filled with pride. My dad made us sing everywhere, he would get excited, and even if he made an effort not to show his pride, it was easy to notice the brightness of his eyes.

I dreamed of singing at school, but my insecurity did not allow me to show the talents I knew I had. Generally, when there were groups at the music school, it was composed of youth with talents just like me, but they had the support of their parents that would go and help them find opportunities. My parents could not give what they never had. Nor was there the necessary communication to alert them of our needs. Today, I can understand it; back then, I had a lot of resentment.

I felt empty, but between the academy and my friends, they filled a big part of that emptiness I had in my life. Out of habit, a week of prayer was held at the academy. In that week, all the students had to meet in the chapel at a particular time. There we sang, and for one hour, we were ministered by a guest pastor. The purpose of that week was for the students to have a different spiritual experience with God.

To be honest, what interested me was that, for a week, I could see my boyfriend sitting on the opposite side, since boys sat on one side and girls on the other. I can't remember exactly how many students, from all grade levels, congregated there, maybe about 150.

It was fun to get there, sit with my friends, and situate myself where I could see who at that time had my heart. I was not the only one, the majority of us went with the same intentions. However, I remember some that were very consecrated and went with a genuine desire to receive and listen to the word of God.

"GOD". That name, at that time, was a "SHOUT OF TERROR" for me; mentioning God was a lot more serious than what you can imagine. In the academy, religion was practiced in a and very careful way.

Because of the experiences already lived, and unlike my peers, I had a way to see GOD. I did not understand how I could worship that "God of Love", the one my dad taught me, spoke to me about his sacrifice, and his care for us, while on the other hand, "mediums" also worshipped and spoke for him, when they were in full "trance". It was impossible for me to make a clear image of "that God" who, back then, had different personalities and characteristics.

It was hard to understand "*that* Love", they talked to me about when I, with barely 12 years, lived in chaos. So, to hear the name of "God" was as if they shouted at my ear and made me jump out of fear.

I was scared because I did not know him. Through the stories that I learned in church, in the, and through the Bible, more than a God of love, to me, was a "VERY PUNISHING" one. I was not happy with him. For me, he was at fault for all my disgrace and for what I was feeling in those moments.

I liked to find the meaning of things, and at that age, I still wasn't clear which side God was on. What was spoken about him did not match with the things he did and allowed. I had thousands of questions running through my head, and if I asked my dad, he would answer based on his beliefs, and if I asked my mom, she would answer based on hers. Way too confusing for me.

Some of the questions that were going through my head back then were: "Why did God take Lucifer out of heaven and left him on earth knowing he was bad? Why did he not destroy him? Also, why did he place us in the same place where Satan was divagating? How was it possible that without asking, I was born and since that moment being in trouble because of a SINFUL nature."?

All these ideas, disagreements, and thoughts continuously ran through my head. It seemed like everyone was looking at a different God than the one I was seeing. The combination of religion, spiritism, divorce, lack of attention, self-esteem, and puberty became a time bomb for me.

I can't precisely remember when the events took place, the day, time, or what was going through my mind. I only know we were at the chapel and the pastor that was preaching was using a mirror that broke in the middle of the message, to show us the point of his preaching and get our attention.

I felt uncomfortable and confused; I tried to tell my friends, but I don't know when I lost consciousness. When I woke up, I was in the infirmary, surrounded by teachers, pastors, and some students. From their facial expressions I assumed something was not right. I asked, and they only said that I had fainted.

I felt a strange sensation; my body was hurting and was very tired. I was amazed to see my dad arrive, besides other people who were from our church but not part of the school. They gave me time to recover, in the meantime, I could see how they went apart to talk to my father and whisper between themselves.

When we were getting ready to leave, as we walked, everyone's gazes at the school were on us. On the way back home, my dad was quiet in the car, his face reflected pain and worry. I tried asking, he only said that I had to remember that God loved me.

When we arrived at the house, there were several people, my mom was lying on the bed, and when she saw me, she jumped, hugged me and asked me if I was okay. When I looked at her, I knew that what was happening had her devastated. She was given a tranquilizer, and they let her sleep.

That night, many people visited us, and all of them prayed for me, even the neighbourhood priest. I just wanted to sleep, felt exhausted, my dad said goodbye, and I was finally able to take a shower to go and rest. While in the bathroom, I looked at myself in the mirror, I saw markings on my back as if I had scratched myself with a sharp object. I assumed that when I fainted, I hit myself.

The next day everything flowed utterly normal. The marks were not there anymore, I fixed myself as accustomed and went out to catch the two public buses, as usual, to get to school.

That day I noticed that everyone was staring at me, something I have always liked, but these looks were different; they were of fear, others of mocking gazes, and others of disbelief. My best friend had her eyes swollen as if she was crying all night. I also noticed that many students missed school.

I wanted to know what had happened, so I asked all my friends, but I don't know if out of fear, protection, or simply because they did not really know what was happening, avoided answering me. They almost convinced me that I was sick, and they were worried about me.

It was time to go to the Chapel, and we sat as we usually do, the difference was that the pastor and the teachers were observing me, and I felt that everyone's eyes were on me. That day and consequently (I have no idea how many more), I woke in the infirmary, always surrounded by many people; on occasions waking up wet, as if water was thrown over me. I always woke up without my shoes, missing parts of my uniform, dishevelled and with a lot of pain in my body.

I remember an occasion where I wanted to go to the bathroom because the pain, I felt in my body was too much, especially on my back. When I went, I lifted my shirt; I was marked as if someone hit me with a whip. I was terrified and did not dare to share it with anybody, or maybe I did, but I do not remember.

Each day there were fewer students, and it seemed that no one wanted to talk about it, throughout the day, I was surrounded by prayer, music, and words of love. They encouraged me to accept Jesus as my personal saviour, and that became a daily priority. My dad, during that week, would pick me up and drive me home. When I got home, the second part of the intercession would start with the priest and other people that were complete strangers to me.

I do not remember exactly how many times that week after my dad left, my mom, in her desperation, would rush me to that house, where she probably thought they could help me.

I remember that they would stand me up front, smoked tobacco and blew the smoke on me and began to call spirits by their names, and everything they did was in the name of God.

They did their rituals and gave me small strokes with plants all over my body. They had lit candles surrounding me. "Mediums" in "trance" would come in and start talking to the spirit that was bothering me. Shouting and hitting the table, they ordained with authority that it had to come out of my body.

No one could ever imagine how that affected my life. In her spiritual ignorance, I could never judge my mother, she understood that was the correct thing to do and the most effective way to help me. For years, I have remembered those scenes over and over. At that time, the fear that was in me surpassed everything, no prayer or word that could take away that sensation I had in me.

I do not know if it was from conviction, convenience or fear, but I accepted to be baptized. Doesn't matter what the reason was, it worked. I do not believe that at the time I understood who God was. I only knew that the influence of the people who loved me, their devotion and conviction, the support of my friends and my parents, were determinant in my recuperation.

For a while, everything was under control. Some things changed a bit; at least my mom never took me to that house again. She continued with her practice, and unfortunately, to control that voice that talked to her, she started taking different pills. She took some for depression, nerves, hallucinations; in the end, she took so many pills that she became an addict to some of them. Over the years, my mom hit rock bottom.

This is the version that I remember of that experience. Without clear details, since I was never able to obtain them, until now.

In order to write this chapter, it was necessary for me to communicate with my beloved friends and sisters, with my former schoolmates, and with the pastors who were present. Many responded to my calling, others did not.

When I started to collect information on what they saw and heard, it was very overwhelming to me, to the point that I could not write for two weeks. It was very hard to listen to my friends retell what they describe a very strong experience, that they would only relive out of the love they had for me, and the desire to help me in this project.

Taking the testimony of the people who were there, since everyone coincides with their descriptions, I will briefly mention, without explicit details, what happened in that chapel.

When the pastor broke the mirror, I fainted, and after a few seconds, I woke up screaming. Several teachers and students had to do an incredible force to take me out of there because I was out of control. They took me to the infirmary. There was a paramedic, and she says that what she saw was incredibly strong and hard to believe.

According to her, and confirming with the other versions, the colour of my skin was different, the tone of my voice was deep and manly, my face was disfigured, my strength was supernatural, and what I spoke was blasphemy against God. It was a hard fight where many people had to intervene to control the aggressions and prevent me from getting hurt. The intention of "that being" was to damage and hurt. His words were of mockery, offensives, and seemed to know very well everyone who was there.

Everyone was convinced that "*that* being" was not me. I was transformed into something supernatural and hard to describe.

Immediately, the teaching staff guided the students and grouped them to pray and to support the pastors that for hours were interceding. My schoolmates, already alerted, knew to follow the instructions, preventing me from finding out what was happening there.

The information that I was able to obtain is very strong and I understand that it is unnecessary to be explicit. I conserved every email with all the details, and I can ensure that even if I wanted to, I could never forget everything I read. Although it was hard, it helped me organize the terrible nightmares I had for years and put them together with all the information I obtained, to have; as a result, a complete scene of what happened there.

I do not wish to give any more details of that "transformation" and of what happened there, because my interest of sharing this story is to show all those people that directly or indirectly, they lived with me that experience, that everything in life has a purpose, even in the things that we, humanly, can't comprehend.

The human being generally to conclude an idea, a story, a situation or circumstance, needs to understand the reasons. Throughout this story, I showed you that there were many reasons; however, it was not the moment for a conclusion.

It was not for me until the moment I started to write this book, that I have the conclusion of that experience. It is not precisely to understand why it happened but to accept the facts, learn the lesson, and overall, share it with the world.

Even if it seems incredible, I feel privileged to have lived that experience that was so hard at the time, and that for years I tried to comprehend. I learned that hell is real, and we all have one. The hell of sickness, mistreatment, abandonment, loneliness, economy, depression, the one of your pasts, the spiritual, and all are necessary to get to know heaven.

You will probably have your own conclusion and determine if that experience was mental, emotional or spiritual. I will leave that to your judgment.

From my part, I can say that it was very clear that there were circumstances that exposed me and made me vulnerable to both parts, good and evil. I feel grateful because, thanks to that, I was able to choose the right path without the fear of making a mistake. I knew on which side my soul ended.

The wisdom of the human being is not based on comprehending what does not have an explanation for us, but in accepting the effects, the impact, and the lessons that it has for our lives. Take the positive out of them and be grateful for the privilege of living special moments that makes us unique and take us to another level.

I dedicate this chapter to all who were by my side. My friends and sisters, apart from what they saw, were never capable of rejecting me, to all who decided to stay quiet before hurting me. Thank you to all of you that responded to my calling and with bravery remembered and shared with me their experiences. Those that for years like me, suffered nightmares and many times cried because they could not understand what had happened. To my parents who were protagonists like me in this story.

Thank you, my God, who beyond my ignorance, weakness, and vulnerability, knew how to take care of me and defend me as a jealous father, giving me the privilege to see His glory, His Power and His immense LOVE, when he conquered me.

CHAPTER 3

When the heart marks your steps

E ACH DAY OF our lives is a "Shout of Alert". We receive signs that indicate to us where we should go.

A few years passed after that spiritual experience. My life was going by pretty normal. In a way and as an instinct of protection, I blocked memories and situations; avoiding them, so they did not keep hurting me.

My mom was still a key point in this stage, she was the person we lived with, and we learned daily from her what was good and bad. When her decisions were not the right ones, we also suffered the consequences.

The day finally came, it seemed that her search for love had ended; the man she thought was the "love of her life" had arrived.

We knew that our parents' love had turned into a fraternal one, of course, it was like that on my mother's side. However, I can't ensure that it was the same for my father, he never spoke about his feelings. They both had the right to rebuild their lives, they had already divorced, and their paths were definitely very different. It was not easy for us to see another man in the house, but we accepted that our mother had suffered a lot and deserved to be happy.

Like every relationship, the first few months were wonderful. He was very tall, brown-skinned, had green eyes, and was very sympathetic. He convinced us to be the perfect man for our mother. After a few months of living with us, we started to notice that he was a little weird; he said and did things that made us think that he was not right in his head. For example, he would lose control if we chewed on gum; he would turn violent and force us to throw it away. He also did not tolerate someone honking at him while driving to make him go faster or move out of the way, that would create a wrath that caused panic.

This fact demonstrated to us that the individual had mental problems. We all noticed, but my mom did not want to accept it, or realize what was evidently a reality.

One of the experiences that hurt me the most was when I was about to graduate from high school, my mom arrived at the school as a surprise; (I believe it was the first time she went). I was in the classroom when the teacher notified me that my mom was on her way to the classroom in pajamas. I got nervous and thought the worst. When she arrived at the door, she asked permission so that I could go to her, so I walked with fear knowing everyone's eyes were on me. When I was in front of her, she slapped my face and said: "This is so you never go back to sleep without washing the dishes". That slap on the face hurt, but what hurt me the most was seeing the grin of that man that obviously enjoyed watching us suffer.

This man knew how to handle and manipulate my mom. In general terms, he successfully managed to control all her life. I did not like the trust and attributes that he would have with me. I was very mature and understood his intentions. I knew that I could not talk to my mom because it would destroy her heart, and if I had told my dad, a tragedy would probably happen. Time passed, and my mom started to become aware and accept that something was now right with him. The relationship was in crisis and he had a behaviour that was out of the ordinary, and so my mom was determined to definitely separate from him.

This provoked him to completely lose control and arrived at our house with a revolver. Between the shouting and the forging, my mom managed to get us out without him hurting us. The police finally took him in custody and this chapter was closed.

About us, what can I tell you? We had already witnessed a complicated relationship between my mom and my dad, and now we were crying and suffering again, but this time we experienced what panic feels like. This experience marked me, but it was too early to understand it. It was not until years later that I realized the impact that it had on my life.

I was always very romantic; although I was very young, I needed to feel that illusion and to have someone showing me affection and worrying about me. Back then, I did not understand, but now I know that my father's distancing and my mother's emotional insecurity, caused an emptiness that I was always trying to fill.

My first love was at the age of 12. He was 17, handsome, intelligent and very studious. I was madly in love, and it cost me to receive punches of all kinds, even with brooms. Obviously, my parents could not accept a young boy of 17 years old that already had a mustache and a beard while I was just a girl.

The story started while I was sitting in the balcony, I would watch him walk back to his house after his baseball games. I saw him very handsome and wanted to know more about him, so I asked my mom if she knew who he was. Obviously, when you are a stylist in the area, you know all the "gossip" of the neighborhood. My mom gave me some basic information, without ever imagining that with that information she had provided me, I would manage to get to know him.

He was a Catholic, very devoted, and everyone even thought he would become a priest. I knew that the easiest way to know him was if I visited the Catholic Church, and that was not going to be hard since some of my friends visited that church. Besides, my dad only came for us on Saturdays, so he would not know that I was visiting the Catholic Church. I had everything well planned.

After some time of visiting the church, one Sunday, they announced the play of "The Passion of The Christ" to be presented during Holy

Week. The people who were interested in being part of it had to sign up. I obviously knew he was going to participate; since he was very active in the church, so I immediately wrote down the date to be one of the first to register.

The big day was here, I was one of the first in line, and they gave me a stellar role to play. The presentation of my character, exaggerating a little, would last about 30 seconds. I was one of the people accusing Peter to walk with Jesus, and guess what? Yes, just as I thought, he was going to be in the play and was given nothing more than the role of Jesus, terrific! He was the protagonist of the play, when and where was he going to notice me? I felt like running away from that place. While he was going to be on stage for almost two hours, I would be there for 30 seconds and that was the most humiliating thing that could happen to me.

My desire to get to know him was way bigger than the humiliation I felt. Since I was never a person to give up, I kept the role without losing hope, that at some time, I would cross paths with him. I was willing to do anything, as long as I achieved my purpose.

At rehearsals, I did not know what else to do to get his attention; I was not having any success. I was about to provoke a cardiac arrest to the one playing Peter. Every time it was my turn to practice my line, I shouted it out; and saw if I was lucky enough to get my "platonic love" to notice me, even if it was for the "shout". Let me tell you, I almost ended aphonic and yet did not achieve anything during rehearsal.

The day of the play arrived; the space was completely full. Even my mom was very proud of the 30 seconds of her daughter. The play was running very well. I did my part, and even if I was dying of nerves, I was not worried because "Jesus" was backstage preparing for his next scene, so to top it off, he was never going to see me act.

Just before the final scene went to stage, where Jesus was crucified and said the "7 Words"; backstage was madness, everyone was running from one place to another, setting up the set, and working in the dressing room. Only the final scene was left, and it was the hardest. They were positioning "Jesus" on the cross. While this was happening, the curtains remained closed. You could hear the background music, and the hammer blows simulating that he was being crucified.

When they were ready to open the curtains, the stage was cleared, and everyone ran to their positions. I was in a corner breathing and sighing, suddenly he steadily looked at me. In disbelief, I looked around, making sure he was looking at me and he said softly: "Run, tell them not to open the curtains".

The cross was already up, and he was on it, with his feet in a base giving the illusion he was crucified. I immediately ran and asked them not to open the curtains. I returned within seconds, and he asked me if I could fix the diaper cloth because it was falling off. I do not know how I did not die out of excitement at that moment! Was he asking me precisely to adjust the diaper cloth? I could not believe what was happening to me. I had to put my fingers inside the diaper cloth and without being able to see what I was doing, I felt the pin that was holding it, opened it, fixed the diaper cloth, and closed it again. Time was up, and they had to open the curtains. I was impacted by the excitement; I felt all my body tremble. I received a miracle.

I have to say the ending was impactful; it brought the entire audience to tears, including everyone who participated in the play. He was a great actor; the agony that Jesus carried was interpreted with pain, sentiment, and very real.

When the scene ended and curtains were closed, they started to lower the cross. Barely without being able to speak, he asked if someone could take the diaper cloth off. inadvertently I had pricked the skin of that lower part with the safety pin. No wonder, his acting was so convincing, he really was under pain. When they asked who adjusted his diaper cloth, I felt the accusing eyes of everyone on me.

I wanted to die; how could it be possible? I was finally able to have contact with that guy after trying for so long, and now, as a result, he was never going to forget me because I was the girl who hurt him at the end of the play.

That night I did my own version of "Cinderella". I ran away as fast as I could and promised myself to never go back to that church. There was a get-together that night for all who participated in the play, and obviously, I did not go. I was devastated and felt incredible shame.

I went to my house crying and told my mom what happened. Of course, for her, it was super funny. I locked myself in the room to cry until falling asleep. I don't know how much time passed, but later my mom entered the room euphoric, telling me to wake up, that "Jesus" came to see me. I didn't know if to cry or laugh, how did he get here? I decided to come out and he was waiting for me with an amazing smile and a piece of cake.

From that moment we started a secret relationship, as I told you guys before, to my parents, he was too old for me. Besides, he did not want people to know he was in a relationship with a girl younger than him. He explained it to me, and I had no objections in accepting. After all, I accomplished what I set out to do. I was with "my prince charming".

In my desire to be closer to him every day, I ended up baptizing in the Catholic Church. My godparents were no less than the directors of the play. They had arrived from Spain, and my godfather was a theatre amateur. He admired my boyfriend very much, more than normal I would say, and in his eagerness to please him, he became my godfather. In that way, we were able to spend more time together.

These people were from a higher social position than I was used to, and with the authority my "godparents" gave them, they subtly began to make changes in my life that inevitably was noticed in my daily behaviour.

They had a beautiful house and prepared a room for me with a white bedroom set. Everything was perfectly decorated. I was super excited and happy because I always wanted to have a white bedroom set.

They signed me up to take modelling and refinement classes, they also took me to see my first opera, and as a matter of fact, I fell asleep. We went to eat almost every day, and all four of us would spend time together. It was definitely the best time of my life.

My dad learned about my baptism in the Catholic Church. Even if he did not question me, his attitude was of pain and frustration. My parents had already noticed the changes I had made, and they were not very happy. One day my godparents spoke with my parents and suggested changing me from school and sending me to a Catholic school. That was the "straw that broke the camel's back," as the saying says. My parents were already distraught, especially my mom, and as I mentioned before, she was not an easy person. Although my mom said a resounding "NO," they asked her to think about it.

Days later, and after my modelling classes, I arrived at my house with my godparents. My mom was furious, and very much at her style, she insulted them, and kicked them out asking them to never come back to get me.

When I saw my godparents leave, I felt that I hated my mother with all my heart. I was hysterical and started to yell at her that she was jealous because she could not give me what they could, among the infinity of many other things.

It was the first time I saw my mom in silence; she looked at me and lowered her head; she gave me an order to go to my room. I went "shouting" and throwing everything that was in front of me.

When I went inside my room, I froze, had no air, I could not believe what I was seeing; there was a beautiful white bedroom set, the most beautiful one I have ever seen. In a second, like a movie, everything I just did was running through my head and shouted at my mom. I felt like dying! I desperately ran, looking for her at her beauty salon that was next to the house. There she was, quietly waiting to see what I was going to say. I ran to hug her, cry over her shoulder, and ask her for forgiveness, I knew I had betrayed my family's love. My mom always worked hard and tirelessly to supply all our needs. Giving me the bedroom set was an act of desperation to rescue me and an incredible and wonderful gesture of LOVE.

I never heard from my godparents. My boyfriend graduated from high school and went to university to study. That left a considerable distance between us, and when he was willing to give me my place in his life and in society as his official girlfriend, he came looking for me, but it was too late. I had grown, and my interests had changed.

Today he is my best friend and confidant. He is a professional holding a position worthy of the efforts of a lifetime. He found the love of his life; he married a beautiful and wonderful woman and is very happy. His life is a success in every sense of the word. That he is happy fills me with satisfaction. I will never know if I made a mistake with not persevering in that relationship, but I was too young to understand the reasons. My life was a continuous race searching for something that, at that moment I could not figure out.

That time was very hard, I suffered the loss of one of my best friends, Zoraida "Zory" Luiggi; for the first time, I felt the pain of losing a loved one. It took me a long time to recuperate. The support of my friends was very important at that time, together we carried that loss, even though we never overcame it.

During those high school years, I fell in love a few times, and each of those relationships meant something different in my life. It was like I needed to have someone for every stage of my life to guide me and show me the way I needed to go.

In seventh grade, I met a charming young boy (JRD), a hard worker, and very spiritual. From him I treasure beautiful memories. He was faithful to God and made an effort to guide me in God's path. He was one of the people who supported me the most in that moment of spiritual confusion. He and his family were vital at that very confusing time; even at a distance they always have a special place of gratitude in my heart.

Already in middle school, this boy (CLM) arrived at the academy. He was very handsome, and with an impressive personality, every girl in the school went crazy. I did everything to get his attention until I made it happen. That relationship hurt me a lot because I was not accepted by his parents, who knew my spiritual and family history. His family clearly let me know.

His parents preferred him to be with a beautiful young girl. She was a daughter of a well known and respected marriage from the academy. The entire family sang and stood out in all areas. She was charming, intelligent, pretty and very loved by everyone. I felt at a total disadvantage.

One Saturday, my boyfriend and I had arranged to meet at the church activity at night. I was super excited. I fixed my hair and was dressed very pretty; I was feeling butterflies in my stomach. Suddenly, almost ready to leave, he called to let me know that he was not going to be able to go to the activity. His mom did not want to take him because she had organized dinner with the other girl and her family.

I felt so much anger, I began to cry without consolation. I did not want to go, but my dad had already come to pick me up. I sat in the backseat, very quiet. It was noticeable that I was crying; a few times, my dad asked what was wrong, without me being able to respond. He kept insisting until, with a lot of sentiment, I asked him, "Why do some people have everything, and everything is so easy for them and others not?" After a silence, he asked me to look back and tell him which was the last car behind us.

I did not understand why he wanted that information. I still looked back and could only see thousands of lights. I said it is impossible to know, there are thousands of cars behind us. He asked again; "Tell me, which is the first car you see at the front?" Being mad, I answered cynically: "Don't you see there are thousands? How am I supposed to know who is first?", he smiled and said, "There will always be someone ahead of you and someone behind you, you will never be able to control that. You must live the best you can and shine in everything you do. That way, you will always have a worthy and unique place to live. Don't worry about who goes before or behind you, that will only stop your steps and will slow you down to reach your goals".

From that moment, I stopped caring what people thought of me. I understood that I was being judged and pointed at because I was different and that was precisely what I liked most about myself. With that illustration, my dad lifted my spirit and learned that it was not worth it to fight for acknowledgments; I knew that I was going to earn it with time. And I did, after a few years passed I earned the respect of his mother and sister.

Unfortunately, a few years ago I heard the news that he had passed away. The impact this news caused me. I will always remember him with special affection and his memories keep him alive within me.

When I got older, I met a young boy (JVF) that was a whole challenge for me. He was not in my school, older than me, and even if he was different from all the youth of my age, he won my heart. If I remember correctly, he was the only one who managed to awaken a real concern in my dad. I had never seen my dad being so interested in this occasion. My dad made our lives very hard, but with time and after a lot of effort, he earned my dad's respect and approval. Today he is one of my best friends. I maintain our friendship and his affection remains intact after the years.

Clearly, you can see I was never alone; I always needed to feel and know that I was important to someone. It was a clear sign that there was an emptiness inside of me that I needed to constantly fill.

My life was not what I desired, but I was used to it. With time, still in high school, I started to work part-time with an orthodontist. In that office, I learned to be responsible and value money. Also, I experienced how difficult it was to study and work at the same time. While the rest of my friends had fun in the graduation activities, I was working.

Those days were exhausting for me; I had to take five public buses daily. After school and work, I would go home to help my mom, who always worked late. So I was in charge of cooking and taking care of my siblings.

Back then I was not noticing that that system of life was preparing me to become a multifaceted person. I did not know the meaning of that word back then, but now I live with the meaning of it.

The day all senior students were waiting for had finally arrived, graduation day. My high school graduation was very emotive. Between laughter and hugs, we said our goodbyes, but yet, speaking for myself, I did not know the magnitude of that farewell. Separating yourself from your long-time classmates and teachers, caused a lot of sadness; many became your best friends and leaving behind that structure that held so many memories was not easy.

I know from ex-classmates who do not share my opinion, they did not have positive experiences at the academy. To them, it was like breaking out from that jail. In my case, it was different; I left behind the only place where I had felt safe for a long time

One time outside of the academy, I realized I even missed the director, who previously seemed to live just to make my life impossible. Many times, until this day, I wish that I could go back to that place where it was my second home and be again with my inseparable friends.

The graduation was a lot more than we imagined. It was the end of a phase and the beginning of a new life. For those who knew where they were heading, it was the biggest moment of their lives. The ones who like me were lost, filled with dreams, but without a defined plan, it was simply a nightmare.

CHAPTER 4

Behind the destiny

I ASKED MYSELF every day, what was I going to do with my life. If you have not decided your plans for the future, when the time comes to decide and choose the profession you will study or what you are going to dedicate yourself to, this becomes a serious problem, and that was my case.

Generally, many people follow the pattern they have seen in their parents since they were kids. If the father is a teacher, they will incline to education; if a doctor, then they will go for medicine. But when our parents do not have any studies or profession of "CLASS," then what generally determines our future are the capabilities and abilities we possess.

Then, there are the people who, since they were kids and without any family influence, always knew with certainty what they would become as an adult. Generally, these people decide for a profession very different from their immediate family.

In my case, I always knew I was never going to be a stylist like my mom; I did not have the ability for that profession. However, I really liked writing like my dad; Still, at that time, I did not have the correct information or anyone to show me which profession went according to my skills. So, it was tough for me to decide my future.

I had just graduated from high school and applied to various universities, being selected by some. It was a blessing to my dad; he was happy to see my desire to study and become a professional. The only problem was that I could not define what I wanted to study, Orthodontics, Journalism, Business Administration, Tourism, or to dedicate myself to what I loved the most… Music.

While I debated what I was going to do with my future, in my house things remained the same, with the difference that we were older, and comprehended the things that were happening in our surroundings.

After my stepdad's departure, my mom, as I mentioned, was in a severe depression for a while. I remember her friends advised her to go out and meet other people, and she did. One day, I woke up to make me something to eat in the kitchen, and I was surprised to see my mom drinking coffee with a friend. It did not seem strange to me to see her drinking coffee with a friend since she generally always had a lot of friends, what surprised me was the way she introduced me to him.

She had let this person know that I had been responsible for the problems she had in her previous relationship. I felt a heat that covered my entire body.

He smiled as if she had said something funny, and I reviewed everything we had to go through and told myself: "No, I am not going through this again."

I gave her the worst look that you can give to somebody, ran to her room, looked for a bag, and then I went to my room and started to pack everything I could. I changed my clothes and walked out of the house very decided and firm.

When my mom saw me, she tried to stop me. She started "shouting" and threatened me that if I left and then decided to return, she would not accept me, accompanied by many insults. As I mentioned, I lived in a commercial area, so the worst part was to see the people walking out of the businesses to hear my mom's "shouts".

I never looked back; as I heard her "shouts," I repeated to myself: I WILL NEVER COME BACK AND WILL NEVER DO ANYTHING TO GIVE YOU THE REASON".

I don't know if I exaggerated or simply took advantage of the opportunity to run away from there; refusing or risking staying and go through what I went through for years of suffering. I was always very impulsive, and that made me a slave of my decisions. I will never know what my destiny would have been if I stayed.

At that moment, the most important thing was to know where to spend the night. I called an ex-boyfriend sister, with whom I had a beautiful relationship. At that time, they were a very united family. From the moment I met them, we developed a beautiful friendship. They always make me feel part of their family. I would let off steam with them, and when my mom was out of control, I would call them, and they always came to rescue me.

On this occasion, it was no different. They came to pick me up, I was destroyed, scared. I was not a person to retract myself, I was very stubborn as I mentioned, so I knew that even if I was dying, I was not going back.

It hurt me thinking of leaving behind my brother and sister. I knew my mom was very upset, I knew her very well and was afraid of her, so the decision was taken. I was not going back; it was time to pursue my destiny.

It was already summer, and I had just turned 17. I resigned my position at the orthodontist office where I was working because I was going to college. So, I had no place to live, jobless, and without knowing what I was going to study and at which university. On the other hand, when my dad learned about it, he came looking for me; he was visibly upset and worried. He asked: "Why did you leave?" I responded: "For the same reason you left", so there was not much he could say. He lived at a senior home, so I could, so I could not live with him.

This family was of great blessing to my life. I stayed a few weeks with them and found a temporary job for the summer. The next step was finding where to live.

It was not easy finding something good, pretty and cheap. It took me some more weeks until I finally found a lodge for young ladies in a great area, although far from the university. The owners were a bit eccentric. Even if it seems absurd, that was the place I was looking for. I knew that the less exposed I was to anything that could distract me from my goals and the promise I made to myself, the better.

Because of my dad I knew my mom was shattered from nerves, taking pills, and very aggressive. It was obviously something very hard for her since she never imagined I could leave my house. Besides her constant emotional changes and strong character, she always loved and cared for us, so it was hard for her.

From my side, I felt free. At that age, we all want to feel capable of making our own decisions without having to be accountable to anyone. Whether we have a dysfunctional or ideal family, the desire to adventure and experiment is part of that stage. It does not always depend on your family or social condition.

The separation from my siblings and my mom put a remarkable distance between us. As adults, we often talk about situations that I, as much as them, lived at that time and never knew. As time passed, we shared those experiences and got to know each other better. Without intending to do so or thinking about the consequences, with that decision, I had divided my family; now, it was them and me.

When we are young, we do not have enough experience to determine what is correct or convenient. In this stage, God also sends us thousands of signals; but the energy of youth dominates the will and generally if we do not have the support or constant supervision of our parents or the people educating us, we will make decisions by impulses and desires, and they will not necessarily be the right ones. Before we know it, we will be like ships adrift without knowing what direction to take.

Leaving my home was a decision that transformed my life completely. Now, I think it was a selfish act on my part because I only thought about myself. My mom was emotionally sick, and my brother and sister were not old enough to help her. I looked for an excuse to run away and go after that completely unknown future to me.

Being impulsive and determined did not imply being insensitive. I cried a lot those first few months, I imagine I had God crazy with all the questions and prayers I did without understanding the signs He sent me every instant.

I had to survive alone; I did not want anyone's help. I needed to prove to myself before anyone else that I could manage my own life.

Now I was in serious trouble; I had financial responsibilities and had to comply with them. While usually, at that age is when you work together as a team with your parents selecting the university and planning your future. I had gone ahead, and completely skipped that stage. Although my parents really, not knowingly, never supported me in that area, I was hopeful that the university was going to be different.

I had to choose where to study and had to do it fast, so I searched for an easy career; after a few tries, I decided on Business Administration. I can't remember how many times I changed faculty that first year, besides changing universities.

Those first months in summer, I had found a place to live and where to go to school; further, I found a summer job where I started to meet a lot of people. I knew the job was temporary, but if there was one thing I learned from my parents, it was always to do an excellent job, so I made a big effort to stand out and win the respect of the adults that surrounded me. As times passed by, I was moving to find another permanent job.

I want to share one of the experiences that I cherish with a lot of love and that completed that summer that was unforgettable for me.

At the summer job, I was not treated like the rest. Thank God they recognized my enthusiasm and responsibility besides my young age, and I ended up working with the Program Director. This caused my working time in that place to be extended more than the rest of the other young people there.

Part of my responsibilities was to make a report for the executive director. That gentleman had his office outside of the area we worked at. But his position and influence were so big, that only by mentioning his name, everyone would run to their positions, including my boss. I remember it was the last week for all the summer employees and as accustomed they did a farewell activity, the "Summer closing". It was celebrated at El Morro in Old San Juan, Puerto Rico.

For the benefit of those who don't know, "El Morro" is a fortress created by the spanish at the time of colonization. It's immense walls protected us against maritime attacks on the XVI century. Today, "El Morro" is one of the principal tourist attractions of Puerto Rico. El Morro has the famous "garitas"; these are small cylindrical sentry boxes with small gaps that allow the Sentinels to do their surveillance. From the "garitas", we can see the immense blue ocean. It is a place filled with real beauty and history.

The day of the long-waited "Summer closing" arrived. Those last few weeks, we worked hard organizing the activity; there was going to be live music, food, and gifts for the participants.

I remember working like never in my life, I was tired and looking to refresh myself. Almost at the end of the activity, I decided to go alone to one of the "garitas" at El Morro. It was distant from the event but close enough to see what was happening. Arriving at the "garita" I went in and felt a beautiful sensation, far from the noise and caressed by the wind; I started looking at the ocean a; I heard the music at a distance. I meditated in everything that happened those past few months when suddenly I was interrupted by a young guy. He didn't look as young as the ones my age, but I knew that they employed the group directors who were between their 20-22 years in summer.

I looked at him, scared. He immediately apologized for the interruption and walked over to look exactly to where I was looking. It seemed strange, but he was so handsome that it was not hard to follow along with the excitement; with a spontaneous reaction, shyly, I moved so he could have enough room to look. Suddenly looking to start a conversation, he asked if I knew the story of the Spanish and the Indian who fell in love at a "garita" at the time of colonization of the island. I found him very intelligent and interesting. For a few seconds I stood quiet and then said: "Yes, I heard of it, why do you ask?", he then started to tell me that he really likes that story and that I reminded him of it because I looked like an Indian. Of course, I told him: "If you wanted to talk to me you could have done it, the little lie was not necessary".

That answer provoked us to start laughing, and for over an hour we were talking about the story of the Indian. Then, he started asking for my name, where I live, and typical questions you ask when you first meet someone. When it was my turn to ask the questions, I heard "shouting's". They were calling me from the activity, so I was scared that I took longer than I should have. I just said bye and left running back to the activity, leaving behind the "garita" and the "sinister Spanish".

On the way back, I felt uncomfortable. The look of all my co-workers was on me, including my boss. He did not look in a good mood and immediately asked: "Is everything ok?" I replied, "Yes, everything is well, thank you", I immediately started cleaning up like everyone else was doing since the activity had ended.

Leaving "El Morro," I discreetly looked back to see if I was able to see that young guy who had left me so impressed, but I did not see him, he disappeared. On the way back, we were all riding on the bus together. My co-workers were making jokes, laughing, and even making fun of me, making comments I did not understand. They were bothering me because they saw me with my new "friend." I barely paid them attention, I was thinking of how silly I was, I never asked for his name.

I barely slept that night, thinking about how good it was to talk to that guy. At the same time, the wind played with our hair, and the smell of the ocean covered us. That music that we heard at a distance, on several occasions, had left us speechless. The only bad thing was that time passed too fast, and I could not know who was the one who had such deep thoughts.

The next day, already back to normal, I started my day very busy. I had to prepare my part of the job, the director's report. That day my boss asked me not to move until I finished, and so I did. Suddenly I see everyone running to their desks, and my boss, visibly nervous, asked me: "You finished?" I said "No, almost done."

At that moment, I saw the young guy from the "garita", with a bouquet of red roses, they were beautiful; I froze. I looked at my boss, and seeing his reaction, I got super nervous, I knew something was not right. In that confusing moment, I did not know how to react; the young boy came in so happy and did not show any shyness. With a firm and sure step, he walked up to my boss, shook his hand, and asked him: "can I take this Indian out for lunch?" I felt a heat that ran through my entire body and before my boss opened his mouth, I went ahead and said; "NO, I can't, can we go outside to talk?", as I pushed him towards the door; I do not know where I got the strength, and in between my teeth I said; "LEAVE! How did this occur to you? They are going to fire me; this is the only job I have".

I remember that he looked at me smiling; it was obvious he did not understand the situation he had put me in. We had everyone's eyes, including my boss', on us and noticing that I told him: "Everyone is looking, please leave". I turned around and ran to my seat, when he came back in and said, "Did you not like the flowers?" I thought, "This guy is crazy! I whispered: "I loved them; can you please leave? I must finish this report that my boss needs to hand over immediately to his "ogre" of a boss, begging him once again to leave.

He smiled like he didn't care about the trouble I was getting into. On the other side, I felt terrible thinking that guy just spent all the money he earned during summer buying me those flowers. Only seconds passed between my thoughts, everyone's eyes and that insistent and daring young guy who remained there, standing in front of me, waiting for me to leave everything, and accept his invitation.

Someone had to react, so indignant I asked him again to leave and explained that thanks to him, I had to go and apologize to my boss. My boss went away to give me space to resolve the situation. Once agains I said to the "insistent" that I had to go talk to my boss, convinced that he understood, I walked as fast as I could until I got to my boss's office.

Incredibly very daring, he came behind me. At this moment, I felt all the blood in my head, I turned violently willing to take him out in any way. Still, he went ahead, and before I could say anything, he asked my boss again if there was a problem with him taking me out for lunch. This was it! I was ready to explode, and just as I am going to react, my boss interrupted and very nervously said: "Not a problem sir. Paralyzed, I exclaimed: "Sir?" Then I looked at the guy shocked and very confused; he came closer and extended his hand to formally introduce himself and said to me: "Nice to meet you, I am that "ogre" (out of respect, I will not mention his name). They started laughing, while without air, in a second, I reviewed all the things he had said.

You can't imagine how I felt at that moment; I did not know if to laugh, cry, or run away from that place. After an exchange of smiles, my boss immediately wished us a good lunch. When we exited the building, his chauffeur was waiting for us in a beautiful vehicle.

What an experience! That guy was the Executive Director of the summer project and many others that ran simultaneously. He had a very recognized position and was well respected by everyone. I heard all summer about him, but he looked so young that I could not imagine all those titles belonging to that handsome young man.

This person was significant in that stage of my life. After a beautiful relationship, we became great friends, and years later was my personal lawyer. Despite how important he was during that time; our lives were moving in different directions.

I didn't know what fear was. At my young age, I already knew what heaven and hell were, so nothing could stop me. I was up nearly every day at 4:00am to walk for 1 hour and a half to get to my job. You can't imagine how many things I had to go through; generally, I would carry a stick in my hand because some sexual predator or a dog would come out to run after me almost every day.

It was not different at night; I would get off from my university at 9:00pm, and if I could not find someone to take me home, I had to ride the public bus. The experiences were as unpleasant as in the mornings.

As fun as my life would seem, it was very hard. Often, I had to wait for my fellow lodging companions to go to sleep to get some of their food from the refrigerator. Other times I ate their leftovers, or simply would not eat.

In this stage, my dad never stopped worrying and supporting me in whatever he could. Almost every Sunday, he came to visit, bringing some groceries and would talk a lot about the university. He always looked for the time to remind me that I had to make time for God. It was still good to see him, although I never told him about my needs or problems I was going through; I did not think it was fair to overwhelm him with my things.

He was the only authorized man to enter the lodge, he was humble and always brought us cookies and games and sat with me and my fellow mates to talk. He was always paying attention to my homework and assignments.

At the beginning of the semester, the university had assigned me to do a report of "Don Quixote of La Mancha." It had to be a profound study where I had to give my point of view on what Miguel Cervantes, the author, wanted to say with this classic. I had to turn it in at the end of the semester as a final grade for my class. I had mentioned it to my dad, and every Sunday, he asked where I was in the book. I had bought the compendium, so I had an idea of what it was about, but that was it. I always had an excuse; I was making him believe I was working on the project.

Months passed, and there were only a few weeks left to present my report. Desperately, I ran to "buy" the report from another student, and my problem was finally solved. I tried to read the book, but to be honest, it was so boring I would fall asleep; I did not see the point of what Cervantes wanted to say. The ingenious "Hidalgo on Don Quixote of La Mancha" had a very confusing way to express his thoughts.

It seemed incredible to me that this novel was one of the most outstanding works in Spanish and universal literature. Especially when I could not understand one word of the message that Cervantes wanted to give.

That Sunday my dad arrived and said to me: "Well, Tuesday is your last day to turn in your report, let me see what you prepared". I froze, it was my dad, and he knew me, so just by looking at him, he knew that "I WAS IN TROUBLE". He said: "I can't believe you are so irresponsible.

That grade is important for you to pass the class". I said, "I know, but I can't stand Cervantes, I DO NOT UNDERSTAND HIM, and it is boring, do not worry, I have everything under control; relax, I will pass the class." Of course, I was not crazy to tell him I had bought the project.

Since my dad is a wise man and lover of classic literature and history, he said: "I want you to sit down and listen to me." Then he started to narrate the story of Cervantes and Don Quixote. He asked: "When you see a crazy little guy talking in a corner, what do you do? Isn't it fun to stop and listen to him?" I said: "Yes, every time I do, it makes me laugh with the craziness?" So, he continued saying: "Then it will be easy for you to understand Cervantes. He knew he would captivate the reader's attention if he used a character who is out of the ordinary and seemed crazy."

I do not know how long it took him to narrate the novel, but he did it with grace and passion. I could not take my attention away; magically, he merged me into the story and brought me to think with Cervantes's mind. His conclusion brought me to tears. I ended up loving Don Quixote, Sancho, and all the characters, but above all, I ended up admiring Miguel de Cervantes.

I remember when my dad finished narrating, he looked at me tenderly, got up and said to me: "Wait for me here." Went to his car and came back with the report, prepared to perfection, and with everything this type of presentation requires. I jumped and cried and thanked him.

Tuesday arrived, and the professor called each student by their last name in chronological order to do the presentation. I was anxious; I had already heard my classmates, and I knew they could not compete with what I had.

It was finally my turn, I remember that I abbreviated, but still wrote every word my dad had told me. When I finished, I noticed everyone was looking at me the same way I looked at my dad. I drove them to understand, in a simple, yet deep way, the message of Cervantes through Don Quixote. The professor looked at me. He sighed and said to me: "So many years studying and studying Don Quixote, and today you taught me to see it from a different point of view that I never thought. Congratulations, I am giving you an A". Everyone applauded, but instead of feeling good, I felt horribly wrong. I did not prepare the presentation, what I was doing was not right. I could not keep a merit that did not belong to me.

So, I looked at the professor, who in fact was a VERY DIFFICULT person. In front of everyone, I said to him: "Professor, I can't fool you. This was not my work, but of my dad", and told him everything I just told you. I concluded my confession by telling him, that passing or not passing the class Don Quixote, Cervantes, and my dad had taught me a big lesson.

I remember everyone was in silence, surprised, and waiting for the professor's reaction. He looked at everyone and said: "You really do not think I notice who has bought the report? You are so foolish that you buy them from the same people". Then he looked at me and said: "You are right, I cannot give you an A, I am giving you both, one for you and one for your dad".

Incredible! I gained the respect from my professor and my classmates; I felt very proud. I remember that next Sunday, when my dad arrived, and I showed him the grade, it seemed I was going to explode out of excitement. He did not to express his feelings, but I perceived that he was very proud of me, and I was super proud of him

A few years had passed, I had gotten used to my life's rhythm. Occasionally, I would see my brother and sister, but I still did not have the courage to see my mom. I knew she was destroyed by her nerves, and I still had resentment against her. I made her responsible for the run away from home that transformed my life.

I got used to being totally independent. I tried to keep myself busy all the time; in that way I had no time to think about what hurt me.

There was a part of my life that was not fulfilled. I remember that in my busy life, I always found room for love. Although it may sound funny now, it was an obvious "SHOUT" from God, showing me that I had to organize the emotional part of my life, which was vital to have a life of fulfillment as I was planning it.

I was the youngest at the lodge; the rest were about to graduate from the university or had already graduated, but they lived far from home, so they stayed there. I was always the "crazy" girl who made them laugh.

I never used drugs, smoked, or used alcohol; I was very firm in my decisions and would not risk giving my mom the reason. But I was completely vulnerable with my feelings.

I needed to feel loved and desired, but I could not decide who I wanted as my companion. Every time I was with someone, I would study every movement and every word, and when I saw an indication or characteristic that brought me bad memories, I would run.

Times had passed and there was emptiness in my heart; I could not fill with parties, university, work, or friendships. I felt tired of living the way I was. Every day I dreamed of a real family. It was my goal; since I was a little, I would ask God how my family would be like, how many children I would have, etc. In the end, I believe we all have the same dream, in my case, I had too much empty space without having someone to give an explanation, I longed to leave my adventurous life.

My childhood and the streets had taught me not to believe in human beings, so I did not count on anyone to move forward. I felt it was a war where I was the only fighting soldier. Each experience was a "SHOUT" of alert, but I was so busy surviving, I was not paying attention to what God wanted to show me.

BEVERLY RUIZ

CHAPTER 5

The marks on my door

MAYBE AT SOME point, you have found yourself in the situation I was in. Some things were easy for me, and some were hard. When you are young, you like to see immediate results, you still have not had the experience to understand that we must learn how to wait and be patient in life. I was very far from understanding it. My desperation to reach my goals did not allow me to reason.

It was always easy for me to relate to people. I had no problem expressing myself, I did not know shyness. It was a great advantage; if I felt like doing or saying something, I would do it immediately. I was always positive and trusted in my abilities very much; this allowed me to easily get where I wanted.

Even with those qualities, I recognized that I have always had a great problem, when it gets into my head to do something, I do not rest until I do it. I think you already noticed that, right. That's how I decided to buy my first car. I was thinking about it for a while, until one day, I woke up and decided to buy the car I always dreamed of. I did not have a specific preference of model and brand, I just wanted it to make things easier. I could not stand anymore to ride on a public bus and go through the bad moments I had to live daily.

First thing was to get my driver's license. I knew my dad so well that before letting me borrow his car, he preferred to be dead, so I looked for my maternal grandfather. He was very special; he always made jokes and was a very happy person. I knew that if I laughed at his jokes, it would be easy to convince him and drag him to my craziness.

The first step was to get my driving permit. I did not pass the first time, but on the second try, I made it. After some time, without driving or practicing, as you should normally do, I persuaded my grandfather to drive me to take the test for the driving license. He did not allow me in any way to drive to the testing site. Once we were there, we filled all the documentation, and I sat waiting for my turn.

When the instructor arrived, my grandfather gave me the keys. We walked to the car, and my test started.

I am sure that no one has ever finished their test in such a short time. Surprised, my grandfather said to me: "Girl, that was fast!" In less than ten minutes, I came back with a paper that said: "FAILED." The instructor, close to a heart attack, approached my grandfather and told him: "Bring her back when she matures." How to forget that day, my grandfather did not stop scolding me the entire way back. I thought the little practice I had was going to be enough to impress the instructor, but I learned that day that manipulation does not always work.

I had little experience driving and learned everything on my own. Generally observing others, I thought that was enough. When I lived with my mom, I would wait for my stepfather to fall asleep and take his car with my brother; I was always daring. Another occasion, an ex-boyfriend had a tow truck with manual transmission; he had an emergency and needed me to drive it. I managed and arrived at the destination without destroying the tow truck.

My last experience driving before taking the test was with one of my fellow housemates. My God! I was crazy. My friend was Cuban and had a medical condition, she was allergic to shrimp. One day, one of the girls and I wanted to go to a concert at Old San Juan and we did not have money to call a taxi, we asked her if she would drive us and she said no. As I said before, I would do anything to get what I wanted.

In this mischief, none of my friends supported me. That day I was desperate to go to the concert and immediately prepared a plan and cooked rice with shrimp. After it was cooked, I removed the shrimp so she could not see them. I prepared everything and made sure she had her pills and waited until she came back from work. I knew her; I knew she would agree to have dinner, so my plan could not fail

She finally arrived, and as I thought, she accepted my invitation to have dinner. I knew she would get allergies, run to get her pills as she always did, and then go to sleep.

That is exactly what happened, as she was eating, she asked me: "What does this rice have? I feel my throat itching." Me, acting as a fool replied: "I don't know, that's strange! Maybe you are allergic to rice"; I even get goose bumps writing this. How did I dare to do something like this? Poor girl! She could not finish eating before running to take her pills. After an hour, she was completely asleep, so we did not have time to lose. We rushed getting ready, made sure she was deeply asleep, took her car keys, and left for the concert.

We came back at dawn, and when I was on the way to her room to leave the keys where she always placed them, there was a note saying: I AM AT THE HOSPITAL.

I almost died of fright; my adventure friends almost killed me, they were hysterical and told me: "We didn't have anything to do with this." But of course, they enjoyed the concert with me! I ran to the hospital and found her completely disfigured. She was being medicated and needed to stay all night at the hospital. I felt so bad! I could only think that if she died, it was all my fault. Obviously, after that experience, I never did anything like that again. She never noticed we took the car. When she went to the hospital, she was so swollen that she could not see and one of the girls who stayed at the lodge drove her. I was twice as lucky that night.

Telling you these experiences, you can understand I never had anyone to teach me how to drive correctly. I learned by myself and observed others. Sometime later, after driving what I considered was enough, I went back and made sure that the instructor was not there. I finally got my license and immediately went to a car dealership; I looked for a car I could afford, meaning the oldest and cheapest they had. It was of manual transmission; that made things a little complicated, but oh well, nothing had been easy for me during the past few years and I kept moving forward, so I would do it again

Because I was underaged, the car had to be bought under an adult's name, so I did not have any other option than spending long hours trying to convince my dad until he finally accepted. We spent long hours in the process of the purchase of the vehicle. Ready to go out with my new car, the dealership did not have any other option than to let me drive it; my dad did not know how to drive a manual transmission

I cannot explain the excitement I felt at that moment. Already in the car, I had to call the seller, when he came close, I asked: "Can you explain to me how to shift gears?" He asked me almost without air: "You do not know how to drive a stick shift?" I said: "Yes, it's just that it has been a long time that I have not done it since I was fifteen".

How to forget my dad's face. He turned red, and when he was ready to jump out of the car, I shifted gear and, in an abrupt manner, went into the well-congested avenue in Hato Rey. Funny! I cannot tell you how my dad's face was. I was concentrating on the gears and to drive without crashing in my new car.

I still remember my dad's shouts, he hardly spoke but, at that moment, he said everything that he did not say his entire life. I finally left him at his house, and taking all the blessing he gave me, I started to venture again in my new car.

Having the car, I was ready to find a full-time job. I started calling some friends and among them the "Ogre Boss", remember him? The young guy from the "garita" from "El Morro"? He had always offered to help me, but I was very prideful and distrustful to receive help, but I did not have an option on this occasion.

A few days after I spoke with him, he called to tell me he found me a job starting immediately with a friend at THE STATE BOARD OF ELECTIONS in San Juan. I was happy! Something was telling me my luck was changing. The next day, I left the house two hours earlier than my appointment because the building was located on a very narrow street, and I still did not know how to park. Thank God I got to the place. After an incredible battle to park, I ran to the building where they were waiting for me.

Following the instructions my friend gave me, no one was supposed to know about this job because it was an accommodation. When I entered the building, the receptionist asked me if I came for the interview, which surprised me. She sent me to the corresponding office and was interviewed by a lady. Then I had to wait for the interview with the boss.

I was surprised when this Cuban gentleman came to receive me, very elegant and serious. I immediately told him I was sent by my friend, but he reacted as if it was the first time, he heard that name. I did not give it a lot of importance and started to answer all the questions he asked. As I had mentioned, I was willing to lie as many times as necessary to achieve my goals.

The first question this man asked after introducing himself was, if I had experience with insurance, I did not understand what the STATE BOARD OF ELECTIONS had to do with insurances, but oh well, I immediately remembered that one of my best friends worked at an insurance company decoding, and in many occasions, I had accompanied her to do work, so I used that information as if it was mine.

Then he started with a bunch of questions relating to my abilities. Among the few that I remember, he asked if I knew shorthand. I responded: "Yes", accounting? "Yes," typing? "Yes," English? "Yes." Bottom line, to this man at 19, I was a complete genius. After evaluating my application, he stood quiet and asked why I wanted to work. Briefly, I explained that I left my house, I was studying and needed to earn more money. That one was true; he said he would call, and I left that place extremely confused. I thought I was starting to work immediately, that was what my friend had told me. When I got to the lodge, I received a call from that office, indicating that I would start working the next day.

My first real job, what joy! Because of my friend's busy schedule, it was hard to contact him to thank him, but I knew he would call.

After a few days working, I finally received the call. He was very upset because I made him look bad and never went to his friend for the job. I said: "Your friend? How can it be possible for your friend not to remember you?" Annoyed, he insisted that the next day I went to work that I looked closely at which building I was working at. Of course, I always arrived very early for work and parked every day in the same spot since it was the only place I knew how to. Then, I would run to the office. I had never noticed the building until that day.

My God! The day of the interview, I entered the wrong building! The State Board of Elections was the building in front of it. Incredible! This mistake had me working fourteen years with the best insurance agent I have met my entire life. He was my teacher, and through his hard lessons, he made me an excellent employee. I learned values and to fight for my dreams. Throughout the years, we repeatedly remembered my famous interview, where to all his questions, my answer was "yes." At that moment, he knew I was lying, but he was moved by my courage and desire to get an opportunity.

Beautiful memories from that time! I worked in every area of the company; I started as a Messenger and ended as a Personal Line Supervisor. As years passed, that man became my second father. From that place, I cherished beautiful memories, and cultivated great friendships. Today, I maintain a great relationship with his children. Like his wife, he left to rest with the Lord; but that distance has not been able to make me forget my gratitude, respect, and admiration. René and Julita, rest in peace!

Already having a place to live, university, transportation, and a good job, something in my heart told me it was time to go back home. Not to live, that would be impossible, but it was time to confront my mom

It was Mother's Day Eve, and I bought tickets to take her to see a show at "Centro de Bellas Artes". I knew it would be a great experience for her since she had never gone before. That Saturday, I went to her beauty salon. While her eternal clients hugged me and flattered me, my mom was immobilized, staring at me. She could not believe I was there, I got close to her, hugged her, and said: "Get ready and look very pretty because we are going out.

Without allowing her to answer, I left immediately before my emotions betrayed me. When I had her in front of me, I knew how much I loved her and how much I missed her. At night I went to pick her up. As always, she was dressed elegantly, smiling, and a bit nervous to see me drive. Her first words were: "Are you sure you can drive?" After laughing, I told her what I had accomplished; she silently listened without any reproach from her or me. We both knew we were wrong, and it was not necessary to mention it.

Here, a new stage in my family life began. God placed everything in its place. It was a relief for me not to live with that feeling of guilt anymore, for being away from my mother, brother, and sister. They were a crucial part of my life, and it was impossible to continue to live away from them.

Everything had changed; I had learned to value what I never found on the streets, the love of my family. Time had passed, and my brother and sister had grown. Although I still spent time with them, we did not go to school together anymore, and their activities were very different from mine. We had missed out a lot. At that time, they looked at me as the "crazy one "of the family, and it was not for less; I was always impulsive and did things no one else dared to do. In addition to running away from home and challenging my mom. That was indeed a heroic act.

Even though I never moved back home, I did start to spend time with them more frequently, and occasionally, we would go out. My mom had fallen in love again and continued to fight to maintain her relationship, something that was always very hard for her. She started visiting the Catholic Church, and her spiritual life was more defined. Unfortunately, she still depended on her medication to control her nerves.

Somehow, even if we never talked about it, we were all doing our part for everything to work out and see each other like the family we were supposed to be. My dad was thrilled to see us spending time together; at the time, the relationship between him and my mother had turned completely fraternal.

Many times, being alone and silent, I asked myself why things happened the way they did. I felt we were "puppets of destiny". I am sure my parents would have never wanted a dysfunctional family, but how to change that? It was a reality, and we could not change the past

We all had a life and a different direction. However, the reality was that, many things were still hurting me. My past was still being present, and I knew if I didn't do something to change that, it would affect my future.

That is why we must be careful with what we do or say with every decision we make. Even if we retract from it or ask for forgiveness, those marks will stay forever in the person.

One time I read a story of a very bad-tempered young boy who had a lot of fun hurting and humiliating others. One day, his father decided to help his son and went to his room with a hammer and a bag of nails.

His son was surprised and with bad humor asked him: "What are you doing here?" To which his father responded: "I came to show you how much damage you are causing." His son, as expected, did not accept he was doing anything wrong. His father challenged him and said to him: "close your room door". With curiosity, the boy closed the door. Then, his father invited him to look at the door and told him: "I brought the hammer and the bag of nails. Every time you offend, yell, abuse, lie, punish, or do something wrong, you hammer a nail on the door. His son, surprised by his petition and with doubts, accepted the challenge.

Few weeks passed, and the son asked his father to go and see how the door looked. When his father went in, he saw the door almost completely covered with nails. With watery eyes, his son said: "Dad, I could not believe I was so wrong, thank you for showing me my faults," and hugged him. The father said: "We are not finished with the lesson yet. Now every time you control yourself and not do wrong, or each time you apologize and ask for forgiveness, take a nail off the door", moved, his son accepted.

After a few weeks, his father went to his son's room, and there he was crying out of excitement. He hugged his father and said to him: "You are the best, thank you; you taught me to be a better person. Look, I have removed all the nails, I learned to ask for forgiveness and control my bad character." The father looked at him tenderly and said: "Son, we are not finished with the lesson, come and sit with me."

After a short silence and both firmly looking at the door, the father continued saying: "Each nail you hammered showed you your faults. Each nail you removed taught you to ask for forgiveness and correct yourself. Now look at your door, how is it?" his son replied: "MARKED".

His father said to him: "It is marked for life, even if you wanted to repair it, it would never be the same as before, it is better not to damage it. Asking for forgiveness makes you feel better, but the harm will forever be marked in that person".

It is a reality, no matter how much of an effort we make to change our faults or ask for forgiveness, the damage is already done. That was precisely what happened with my family. There were too many marks in each of us. There were too many marks on our door.

At that time, I was still too young to understand the consequences of those marks in each of us. It was all a matter of time.

CHAPTER 6

Dreams in white

I WOULD NOT dare say that every girl's dream is getting married to their "prince charming", like in fairy tale stories; but I did. I remember going to sleep, imagining how my wedding would be like. Of course, with time, I understood that the "prince charming" is only a story. I had many suitable lovers, but from that to "prince", there was a big difference.

It is tough to believe in love and princes when we grow in dysfunctional families. Beside my experiences, I had hope of building the home I always dreamed of. I wanted to prove to myself that true love did exist.

I was always a very confident person. In general, when I noticed someone, I considered special, I always ended up getting their attention, and often stealing their hearts. I did not like to be alone, there were very few times where I did not have a relationship in my life. I must confess that it was hard to maintain stability in my relationships because I got used to being completely independent. I did not need someone to maintain me or to manage my life. I only needed someone who loved me, respected me, and fulfilled the ideal prototype of the man I had dreamed of.

When I thought about my ideal man, I imagined him PERFECT, attractive, tall, elegant, intelligent, sympathetic, educated, comprehensive, romantic, detailed, talented, sensual, sexual, hard-working, athletic, spiritual, considerate, always ready to listen, understanding, and with an incredible personality. It was, in my mind, the only place where that "perfect" person could exist, the one our grandparents called "soul mate," and who I called "the man of my dreams," "my prince charming".

I am sure I am not the only one who has dreamed of their ideal man or woman. We all have in our mind the prototype of the person we understand would be our perfect match. Many times, we let real opportunities pass waiting for that "ideal person," who generally we will never find.

As time passes and after suffering disappointments and frustrations, we understand that we will not always receive exactly what we are dreaming of. Since we are little, we dream about the qualities of that person that will be perfect for us. Rarely, if not "never", we think of the defects or limitations that an "IDEAL" person could have. So, once we choose the person that gets the closest to our specifications, after a while, we start discovering that they were not so perfect as we imagined. Not because we dream about what we call "happiness," it means that it will make us happy.

I know many people that spend their lives dreaming and waiting for that as an "act of magic". Everything they have dreamed of arrives just like in movies and has a happy ending. I am sorry to tell you; it will not be like that. In reality, happy endings are circumstantial and not predictable.

What is a dream? It **is a desire, event, or condition that you hope for very much, although it is not likely to happen;** this is the definition in The Cambridge Dictionary. It means that when we dream, we are desiring something that we know we can't obtain at the present time. I was always convinced that any dream could come true if we wanted to with all the desires of our hearts and worked to reach for it.

But speaking about love and choosing the "ideal" person was not as easy as I imagined. I thought that the fact that it was easy for me to relate and had fallen in love a few times, that it capacitated me and made me an expert to be able to identify the perfect person as soon as I had it in front of me.

I was 20 and four of those years living independently. Those two factors made me believe I knew it all. That was a great problem. Although I had lived advanced experiences at my age that made me mature in certain areas more than other young people, I still had a lot to live and learn. Of course, at that moment, I was convinced of the contrary. My ignorance put me at risk of making mistakes very easily.

I longed to know what having a family meant, and felt it was the moment to build it. I already had a good job, a car and was in university, so the time had come to choose that special person I would spend the rest of my life, and just as I dreamed of. I wanted to find him quite like that prince charming that for years I imagined

I was used to planning everything and even preparing an immediate strategy to achieve my purpose, so it was no different this time. I started working on my plans. The first thing I did was make a list of all my suitors; there were a few interested. From the list I chose the one I liked the most "physically." That was the biggest of my defects, I always preferred the most attractive man.

After eliminating half of the list, I started looking at who aspired and was nice and intelligent. Little by little, I shortened the list.

Although it was difficult for me to define my feelings, I was very clear that I would never be involved with an older man. In my subconsciousness, I refused to live what I had seen in my parents' relationship. I would never be with someone with an addiction, whether it was alcohol or drugs.

Incredibly, my plan, strategy, and "experience" and that supposed discernment and capacity to identify the perfect man were useless. The list, the analysis of each one of the prospects, were also meaningless.

That's right… One day I met this tall, handsome, and very timid guy. He was not part of my circle of friends. As an act of magic, and without enough effort, he won my trust and heart in a short time.

He was QUITE THE OPPOSITE of all the other prospects. He had not finished school, was divorced, had a son, and had just moved from New York to Puerto Rico. He came from a humble and simple family.

What impressed me about him? Besides his looks and personality, maybe his past and what he had endured getting married so young. He was very reserved, and very few times, I knew what he was thinking. But he had something in common with me, his desire to build a family. When he was very young, he left his house and lived at a distance he lacked and suffered many needs. Now that I think about it, it was the only thing we had in common. That moved me, and I think the first feeling that was awakened was one of compassion and tenderness. Back then, it seemed like enough to decide to build a life with him.

After a short time of meeting his family, I decided to introduce them to mine, already convinced that he was the chosen man. I remember Thanksgiving Day. My dad, as he always did, came to my mom's house very early in the morning bringing the turkey and all the traditional food for this festive day.

I was very nervous and anxious. His family finally arrived; it was a full house. Even my maternal grandparents were with us. As soon as they walked in the house, after a shout of excitement, my dad and his mom hugged and jumped with joy, we all looked at each without being able to say a word; they were cousins. After this family reunion, it was imminent that I had to begin with my next step, "the wedding."

As I accustomed, I began preparing a plan. Before the wedding, I wanted to have my own house, so I started searching for the ideal home to start my new life. Like I have been telling, my worst defect was being impulsive, which took me to do what I thought or desired immediately at any cost.

When we found the house, one of the requirements to be able to buy at that time was to be married. I did not want to get married until I had everything as I proposed myself.

I remember I managed to supply the bank with all the requirements they asked for, including the Certificate of Marriage. Since you should already know me, I even falsified that. If I remember correctly, the only real information in that transaction was my name and signature. So once again, I achieved my purpose based on lies and pure mess.

It was never going to be possible to buy the house if I had told the truth. Already having my new home, the next step was "THE WEDDING".

The long-awaited day arrived. I took some time to organize it and took care of every detail. It would be a very simple wedding, but with all the elements this ritual carries. While my mom was fixing my hair and helping me get prepared, I could see on her face the joy of seeing that I was getting married as she had once done. My dress was very white with embroidery; back then, the fashion was "pamela hats," it was nothing more than a sun hat decorated with pearls and a veil that ran to my mid-back. I wore white gloves and simple makeup.

When I looked at myself dressed as a bride, I felt mixed emotions. I was in the room I once abandoned. Everything was intact, my white bedroom set, it seemed as if I never left. My mom, the one that at one point I could not seem to understand, nor she understood me, had dressed me with all the love and sentiment of a mother at her daughter's wedding day.

I looked at my reflection in that mirror and I did not know if it really made me happy. I felt confused, scared as very few times I had been;

but at the same time, I felt it was a new beginning, it was the moment to leave behind everything that had hurt me before.

As my dad and I waited for the signal to start the walk to the altar, with immense sadness, he asked me if I was sure of the step I was taking. If I was marrying for the right reasons, I replied yes, I was sure.

When we started walking to the rhythm of the wedding march, coldness ran through my entire body. It confirmed that I had made a mistake; within seconds I reviewed all the reasons that had taken me there and I discovered that they were not the correct ones. I could not retract nor hurt that guy and his entire family.

Firmly, I followed my step and never during the whole night I had the courage to look my dad in the eye. He was the only one to perceive what was inside of me. He knew I had made a mistake, but he also knew that I would never back down from my decision.

June 23, 1983, my dream to be dressed in white was fulfilled. I provoked things to go as I planned. With time, I learned I could plan to buy a house, but not a home. Plan to find a husband, but not love.

We were both very young and had suffered living away from our homes. We went through hunger, coldness, loneliness, and we both were emotionally mistreated. These reasons made us vulnerable, and if I add to this the typical passion of the age, it was very easy to confuse the emotions.

There were beautiful feelings between us, but it was not enough for the most crucial step of our lives. Despite my feelings, and what that voice shouted very deeply inside of me, I became the wife. I had decided, but even then, I did not know the magnitude of the consequences.

CHAPTER 7

Slaves of our decisions

ACCORDING TO THE Cambridge Dictionary, slavery is defined as:

"It applies to a person who is legally owned by someone else and has to work for that person, has no personal freedom."

Another version says: Rigorously or harshly subdued to work, passion, affect, etc., Deprives liberty. *Man, slave of his Word, ambition, friendship, or envy."*

For years society, government, and human rights defenders have fought tirelessly for the freedom of slaves. When we speak of slavery, we immediately think in chained people deprived of their freedom, doing forced work, subdued to the control and will of someone or of an entity.

In the XXI century, where you and I currently live, Slavery is not supposed to exist, as we learned in history books. But unfortunately, we are still living in a silent slavery. Human trafficking, labor abuse of immigrants, sexual exploitation of children and women, etc. In fact, I could mention thousands of examples of modern slavery with are living in.

Maybe it is not in your hands to change this sad reality, but I want to talk about a slavery that has probably affected you just like it has affected me, from which I hope you can set yourself free as I did: our DECISIONS. In general, we make decisions thinking of present circumstances without considering that it will determine our future, becoming slaves of our own selves. The insatiable desire to please ourselves or to please others, often drives us to make decisions that will make us slaves of our consequences.

I am a living example of being a slave of my decisions. Even knowing I was getting married for the wrong reasons, I insisted in following along with the plans. My emotions and fear were stronger than my reasons and logic.

The social pressure or our family pressures are generally stronger than the reasons. When you already decide, you share it and involve others to participate in your plans; then, you provoke the pressure of compromise. Simply stated: "What will they say?", are only 4 small words, but the weight and impact of them in our lives will be incalculable.

"What will they say?" If you take a few minutes to analyze your life, you will realize that most of the decisions you made or never made were based, thinking of others and not necessarily yourself. I was an example of that. From the beginning I had the emotional pressure of my mom, the fact that she "shouted" at me the day I left my house that I "would return defeated and pregnant" had various effects in my life:

#1: I challenged myself to take care of every step I took to avoid giving her the reason.

#2: I made decisions I knew would make her and my dad happy, but not necessarily made me happy.

In other words, I had become a slave myself. Those words had the power to control my actions and decisions; I never did anything to change it. It made a plan based on what society stipulates as: "the right steps we should take to live in order and acceptance," and I followed them to the letter, forgetting about my feelings.

Right before entering the church, I had the opportunity to back down and say, "You know what? I don't want to get married and I won't do it." Unfortunately, at that moment, the four magic words came into action: "What will they say? What will my parents, friends, boyfriend, and all who had been invited to be part of this compromise say?

So, in that instant, I preferred to take the risk and continue with what was stipulated, instead of filling myself with courage, defending my reasons, and facing pressure from everyone. Pressure, that, would have been less painful than all the consequences I had to face later.

This reminds me of the circus elephant, who, since very little, was chained to a small stake buried in the ground. Since he was little, he tried with all his strength to get away and never succeeded. Until one day, terrible for his story, the animal accepted his impotence and gave up to his destiny. That powerful and enormous elephant we see at the circus does not escape because he thinks he can't. He has engraved the memory of that impotence he felt shortly after being born. The worst part is, he has never questioned that memory. He never tested his strength again.

We all are kind of like the "circus elephant" and go around the world tied up to hundreds of "stakes" that deprive us of freedom. We made ourselves slaves of our own decisions because we convince ourselves that we cannot change the reality we are living.

In my case, I was married and had to resign myself to the idea that my freedom and many of my dreams had to be left behind to fulfill the role I had accepted. Of course, I was still very young and did not understand that it did not necessarily have to be like that; but like the elephant, I resigned to live a life that, at some point, was part of my dreams.

Like in any relationship, the beginning seemed to be perfect. We had no luxuries, but we lived quite well. However, there was something that felt awkward about my partner and, at that moment, I did not have the maturity to understand the seriousness of what I was beginning to discover.

Being a mother was not my passion, so I went to the doctor to get birth control. As they normally do, they did a general check and a cancer test. After two weeks they contacted me and asked me to go to the doctor's office as soon as possible. Despite my insistence, they did not want to give me any information, but I was told it was necessary that I went immediately.

It was obvious something was not right. I remember that my husband, very tenderly, supported me and gave me words of consolation. It was not enough to stop this sensation that ran through my body.

We arrived very early at the doctor's office. He saw us and gave us the bad news; I had CANCER in the uterus. We stood cold, I could not believe what I was hearing, how could that be possible? I was still very young and had no children. The doctor said that the good news was that it was in just one place. With a small surgical procedure, he would remove the affected area, and everything would be alright. Although his words gave me relief, the word CANCER provoked concern and panic.

Two days later, the doctor performed the procedure. I will never forget the incredible support I had from my husband and my parents, especially my mom, who never left my side until everything was over.

The most difficult part was the recovery and not knowing if I would become a mother one day. The doctor put me in a fertilization treatment, although he could not guarantee it would work.

Incredibly, after six months of treatment, I was able to get pregnant. I cried, shouted, jumped, and the entire family celebrated. I thanked God every second for the privilege He had given me.

BEVERLY RUIZ

From that precise moment, my life completely changed. Knowing that there was life inside of me had changed my focus. It was not about me anymore, now my fight was for that being that had become the reason for my existence.

Back then, 28 years ago, there was no advancement in technology like we have now, and according to the doctor, I was having a girl. I was happy, I bought everything and decorated the room for a girl. We even chose her name, "Jennifer Shinee," even at the baby shower, everything was directed and dedicated to "Jennifer".

Very tense for the birth and trying to prepare ourselves for the event, a few days before we went to practice the route we would take to go to the hospital. The suitcase was ready right by the bedroom door. I missed the indicated due date, but the doctor said it was normal with first-time mothers.

One night, I started to feel those unbearable pains; I remember that I called everyone as if that helped me to feel less pain. Early in the morning, my husband was deeply asleep, I woke him up with shouts, I couldn't take it anymore, although my water was not broken, my body was releasing something I had never seen before.

He woke up with my shouts and told him: "Run, the time has come." I had my doubts that he was awake since he looked a bit confused and did not know where to go. Finally, and after coming out of the bathroom, he got dressed, took the suitcase, and left. I could not believe what I was seeing: HE LEFT ME BEHIND; after a few seconds, he came back and said: "I am sorry, I am asleep and nervous". I almost killed him! The pain had me out of control.

He helped me get in the car and we left for the hospital. I remember he took all the holes he found on the road; between my shouts and insults, I had him so confused, we went around two or three times to find the hospital's entrance. You can't imagine how happy I was when

I saw that hospital entrance. After a few hours of unbearable pain, the doctor decided to proceed with a caesarean section. To top it off, my uterus was reversed, making it difficult for the baby to come out the natural way. What a joy I felt! That anesthesia made me see the "Glory of God." Finally, those unbearable pains had left.

What a wonderful experience! That is the moment when we are the closest to God. Only a mother can understand the excitement being felt when you hear your baby cry for the first time. Only a simple sigh and a comment from my doctor took me out of the emotional "trance" I was in. The doctor cleared up his throat and said:

- OH! OH!

- I got scared and asked him: Doctor, is the baby girl ok?

-He told me, that is the problem, "It is not a girl!"

-What? The only thing that occurred to me to say: "I WILL CHARGE YOU FOR THE ENTIRE DECORATION!"

I felt horrible. I felt disappointed and, for a few seconds, lost the excitement until the nurse put my beautiful baby on my chest. I forgot about the girl and looked at the beautiful face of my baby boy, that little one had changed my existence

Of course, I must be honest, I had everything for a girl and many things were impossible to change; so, when I was home alone, I dressed him in little dresses and bows. That part, he probably won't be happy that I share it with you.

Our son had become the center of our lives. Still, he could not fill or put in order the reality of the relationship between his father and me. Each day, the relationship was being affected more. The financial problems were more evident with the arrival of the baby.

The stage of the excitement passed, and now, we faced reality. The consequences of my decision were starting to be seen. He was weak spiritually and emotionally, that was the reason for my union and the reason for my abrupt separation.

He made a very drastic change. He maintained a depressive attitude and that drove him to use drugs; once I discovered that tendency, immediately without giving him any opportunity, or trying to help him, I decided to separate. It was something my system blocked. My past experiences did not allow me to tolerate or manage a situation like this.

It was the excuse I used to escape from a situation or relationship that maintained me submissive and without will, like the elephant, thinking there was no way of changing it.

There were hard moments, fights, reproaches, resentments, and I never gave in to give an opportunity.

I remember long nights crying and asking myself, what happened? This was not what I dreamed of. How did I get here? I ended up selling the house and practically empty-handed with a baby, I decided to move forward as I always did. Now I had a stronger motive than myself, I had a son.

As years passed and thousands of situations and sufferings, that ex-partner left for California with a great woman who helped him move forward. Today we maintain a cordial relationship, and he maintains a beautiful relationship with his son and grandchildren.

He found true love; this made a big difference in his life. He overcame all situations, depressions, and was finally able to find his way.

We all have options in life, you decide and determine how you will live your present and your future will depend on it. God talks to us from within and often "shouts" at us to wake us up and bring us to our senses, but He cannot obligate us to decide.

For many years, I was a slave to my impulses, and decisions. I dragged other people along to suffer the consequences with me, but I knew that unlike the elephant, I WOULD NEVER STOP TRYING.

CHAPTER 8

Success or failure?

O NE WAY OR another, we all have experimented with failure. Nobody likes to lose. But what is failure really? It is the opposite result of what you hoped for.

We have different ways of seeing failure, depending on which stage we are living in. When you are a student, a failure can be less than 69% in a test, and success is more than 70%. With time, you learn that failure is not a percentage or a test, but a process.

It is more common and easy to fail than to have success. But we all know that reaching success or our goals, it requires a process and we generally fail several times before reaching what we hoped for. Failure is the step prior to success.

Just to mention a few of the well-known people who knew success before failure. Is very well known that for 28 years, Abraham Lincoln experimented failure after failure before being elected as The President of the United States of America. Walt Disney was the same way, failing on a few occasions before having success. Albert Einstein and Werner Braun failed their math courses. Henry Ford was bankrupt at 40 years old. The teacher of Thomas Edison called him ignorant. Then, Edison failed in more than 6,000 occasions before perfecting the first electric light bulb. They all had to fail more than once to be able to reach their goals.

Enrico Caruso said: "Failure is an event, not a person." It does not matter how bad or how many times a person fails, he is never a failure if he gets up from the fall." It comforts me to know that the most important people of our humanity had multiple failures before they reached success.

Having this principle clear in my life, I knew that chapter of my divorce was closed, and I was ready to try it again and take the chance to succeed or fail.

After some time, I decided to retake my life and start over. I remember a friend invited me to go out to the club I used to visit before getting married. I accepted the invitation. I left my son in good care, and that night I went out facing an environment that this time was completely unknown for me.

I felt out of place being at the club, the music, the style, and everything had changed. While my friend danced, I settled in the darkest corner I found hoping that no one could see me. Surprisingly, a man invited me to dance, he was tall, had green eyes and super elegant. His accent was foreign. After sharing time with him, I recognized that he was a very well-known person in the artistic environment, besides being a known athlete.

Completely amazed, I asked my friend, "How could it be possible for that man to notice me?" I had a wonderful night. He asked for my phone number, and when I gave it to him, he did not have where to write it; I thought after all the glasses of wine, he would never remember my number, let alone my name; however, he promised me he would remember.

On the way back home, I was on a cloud. To me, he was the most handsome and interesting man I had ever met. The next day I received the awaited phone call. I almost died of excitement. I made the biggest effort to answer neutral and not let the excitement I had to be noticed.

We had a brief conversation, and days later, he came to visit me at my house. After a short time, I was convinced he was my "Prince Charming."

We started to spend time together and get to know each other better. Each day I convinced myself that while to me, he was my "Prince Charming," for him I was only a special friend who occasionally made him company and filled his passions and desires.

Many times, in our conversations, he let me know clearly what type of woman he was looking for. In the specifications, there was one who clearly left me out of the competition. He wanted a woman who had the same social status. I was very clear he did not have the remotest idea to have something serious with me.

As it has happened to many of us, we expose ourselves again and again without paying attention to the very clear, because we hope for something to change. That one day, as in fairy tales, that person wakes up convinced that you are the great love of his life.

I spent a year between sporadic dates and calls. On many occasions, my friends saw him with the company of other women. I did not have the facility to go out because I had my son, so whenever he called, I would make him think I personally saw him. When he would ask why I did not greet him, I would say: "I couldn't because I also had company. "What a fool! IGNORANTLY I thought that this way I would set clear that he was as important to me, as I was important to him.

Falling in love with him, getting my hopes up, and sleeping with him were not the worst mistakes I made, but rather making him think I was a modern and liberal woman. While he imagined me having fun, I was in my house crying out with rage and waiting for my phone to ring so I could hear his voice.

I did everything that I could come up with to get his attention. I started riding a bicycle, running at the beach; in short, I looked for the minimum excuse to be able to get close to him, and I generally succeeded.

"Life gives you surprises;" I give faith to that saying. Surprisingly one day riding the bicycle and almost to the meeting point with my friend, I felt dizzy and ended up unconscious on the floor. I felt very sick, but my financial situation did not allow me to see a doctor, so one of my best friends and wife to a well known gynecologist, insisted I examined myself with her husband.

That was one of the most difficult decisions I have ever had to make, can you imagine? My best friend's husband, my gynecologist? But oh well, I did not have an option and went to see him.

That visit was all an adventure. I will never forget that after my friend did the routine interview at his office, he asked me to go to the examination room. I wanted to die of embarrassment. His wife was in the room and his secretary, both my inseparable friends and sisters. Did it make it easier? No, quite the opposite, it was harder. I remember in between their laughter I laid on the bed. Once I accommodated myself, he entered the room very professional, and at that precise moment I changed my mind and SHOUTED: "No, forget it, I'm leaving!" He stopped me trying to convince me to see him as my doctor and not my friend while my friends were dying of laughter. Finally, covering my face, I surrendered at their insistency, and he was able to complete the examination.

To facilitate the moment I was going through, he asked me to get dressed and call him over the phone to explain the results. My doctor confirmed that I was PREGNANT. I will never be able to explain everything I felt at that time. I was going to be a mother. That was impossible, I COULD NOT have children unless I had a treatment. Four years had passed, and I never got pregnant again.

I was going to have a child from that man to whom I was completely insignificant. In my desperation I thought the worst; I did not know how I was going to be able to maintain another child when I could barely maintain the one, I had.

Ironically, I cried; I refused and fought with God as if it was His fault. Four years prior, I also fought with Him because I wanted to become a mother.

God is God, He knew us before we were born. I assume He did not pay attention to me and took me through the path that was going to be hard, but necessary to reach another level as a woman, mother, and human being.

As expected, the reaction of this man was dreadful. I know that until this day, he believes I premeditated and planned this pregnancy with the idea to retain him by my side.

It was a very hard process, I did not have money, and many times, the food was only enough for my son, and I had to go to sleep hungry. My friend and her husband took care of all the delivery expenses. I do not know how I would have made it without their help. The baby was huge, and my body could not handle the weight, I could barely walk. My poor four-year-old son helped me with everything he could.

My health condition and the baby's weight provoked a considerably early arrival. They had to do an emergency caesarean section. As I waited to be taken into the delivery room, I cried and felt very guilty. I was terrified that things would not go right with my baby. It was a premature delivery and was very risky.

Looking for strength, I remember asking the doctor if my friend or someone had come to the hospital, and very serious, he replied, "No, no one has come. "The nurses prepared me, and when they were taking me to the delivery room, they took me to the hallway. I had an incredible surprise, they were all there, my friends, family, neighbors, and even bosses. It was wonderful to know and remember that I was not alone.

The caesarean section was not easy; I had problems with the anesthesia and was under a lot of tension. I finally heard my daughter cry. They quickly put her on my chest and was able to see how beautiful she was. She was a big baby; her skin was very white and did not have much hair. I was barely able to see when they had to take her.

While in the recovery room, I vainly remember the pediatrician entering to give me the bad news. My baby had serious problems. She was born with pneumonia, a heart murmur; besides her kidneys and liver were not ready and not functioning how they were supposed to.

The doctor promised to do everything possible to save my baby. When the doctor left, the pain and desperation left me without air. I just wanted to get up and see my baby; this provoked my anesthesia to go to my head and almost went crazy with the pain

As expected, my baby had to stay at the hospital under intensive care. I was only able to see her from a distance, I was never able to hold her, breastfeed her, or even see her with her eyes open.

Only God and the mothers who have lived this experience can understand the immense pain that is felt. The impotence of not being able to do anything to help that little being that came out of you. A few times, we tried to contact the father, but he never responded. My pain was doubled and hard to explain.

But God had a purpose with that baby, and her strength kept her going, and after a few weeks, I was able to hold her in my arms for the first time. When I looked at her, I could not believe what I was seeing; her eyes were bluish-green and matched perfectly with her skin color. Incredibly, that baby did not have any of my looks; she looked exactly like her father.

Time passed, and I was recovering my dignity and the strength I lost during all those months. Once recuperated and leaving behind my limitations, I decided to fight for my daughter's rights, achieving that my daughter be legally recognized.

Currently, the relationship between my daughter and her father is cordial. The years along with the different stages passed, and we could not stop them. My daughter was the most affected in this story. She will always miss not having a close relationship with her father; however, my experience taught her not to make the same mistakes I made. She is currently happily married with her "Prince Charming," she indeed made it.

Was it a failure? No, not at all. It was a learning experience in every area. This experience made me comprehend we can never play with our integrity and dignity. There were many times I made that man believe I was with someone else in the same place he frequented, as vengeance? For his attention? Out of pride? Whatever the reason may be, it was wrong.

This only provoked him to doubt my morals and that the process to be hard, affecting both of us, especially the baby, who, in the end, was who suffered the consequences.

I learned very abruptly that we can never feign or pretend who we are not, with the intention to achieve our purpose. The person who is going to love you will accept you as you are. When the love is real, it is not conditioned to social status, culture, or skin color. Love simply is born and flows.

Besides, we cannot assume and wait to be reciprocated without looking at the reality in front of us. I still had a prototype for my "Prince Charming." I saw a few qualities in him that made me give in with all I had in exchange for nothing, believing that one day I was going to obtain his "love."

Love cannot be planned. We cannot "IMAGINE" that we will be loved and wait to see results. God gave me many signs; He spoke to me and I still paid attention to my emotions. We must be careful with our emotions; they are often HALLUCINOGENS, making us lose perspective of reality. I did not have the expected results in love. In my daughter, I conquered victory and divine reward.

I thank God for this experience, and I expose it in my book to encourage all those men and women who are searching for the love of their lives. BE CAREFUL! We must learn how to love with reason and not emotion, to make the right decisions and have positive results.

I dedicate this chapter to all those who supported me, who cried with me and who along with me and my daughter fought for her rights. I especially thank the support of Isabel and her husband Dr. Manuel Velilla; I will never forget so much love. My family, who unconditionally was always by my side. To my beloved and inseparable friends and Erickson and Amada who were an important part of this process. But especially to all those single women who are fighting alone to raise their children. Today, in the midst of the battle and the process you might have many questions as I did one day. You will have the answers when you hear your baby's first cry.

-Failure is not the end, is the beginning of the Victory-

CHAPTER 9

The angel with the blue duster

I SPENT MOST of the night crying on the balcony, I could feel the breeze of the ocean, it was only a few steps away from where I lived. I had taken some time, but I had decided, and there was no going back. For hours I looked at my little one's sleep, I asked them for forgiveness, and kissed them again and again, but at that moment, I was convinced they would be better without me. At sunrise, and with my heart destroyed, I took them to care and said goodbye. I left without consolation.

I decided I did not want to continue living. I did not see an exit to the situations that were consuming me. They had me completely surrendered and defeated. I went to buy the pills, and next to the pharmacy was a library. They had a table full of books at the entrance, and an elderly lady with a blue duster shaking off the dust from the books. When I walked by her, she said: "Wait, I have a book that can help you. "I did not want to stop, much less to see a book I would never read. I did not want anything to distract me. It had taken me a long time to make the decision, and I had to do it before losing courage.

I accelerated my steps, but the elderly lady came behind me; she stopped me and insisted again: "Come, let me show you this book." I knew she would not let me leave, so I accepted, letting her know I was in a hurry. She took me to where the book was, took a copy, and placed it in my hands. The title of the book was "LIVING, LOVING AND LEARNING" from Leo Buscaglía, a writer born in California from

Italian parents. Professor and professional motivational speaker, better known as Dr. "Love."

Although the title impacted me, I thanked her and told her I would buy another day. I did not think I had the cost of the book, regardless. But the lady insisted, she said it was only $11.99. At that moment, I knew it was the only way to free myself from that sweet, kind, and very insisting lady was buying that "blissful book."

I searched my purse to see if I had enough money. Meanwhile, the elderly lady was looking at me, convinced I would take the book. I had exactly $12.00. I paid for the book, thanked her, and ran from that place.

I got to my apartment with immense sadness and opened the sliding door to feel the ocean's breeze. It was a beautiful day. I took the pills out and put them on the table, I looked for the letter I wrote during the night letting my family know the reasons and instructions to follow with my children. I served a glass of water and placed it in front of the pills.

I grabbed the phone and called my mom. She was working, but with my tone of voice, she assumed something was not right. I told her I loved her and tried to convince her that everything was in order. I finished the call, cried, and shouted again as if I could find a reason to not take that step that was already imminent.

I put all the pills in the palm of my hand, and when I was ready to put them in my mouth, I reached for the glass of water, and just next to the glass of water was that bag with the book. Something caught my attention, and with sobs, I put the pills on the table and opened the book.

In less time than I imagined, I had read half of the book; I was not crying anymore, and without finishing it, the decision to take my life had changed. I don't know how long it has been. I submerged myself in that reading like someone who has been in the desert without water for weeks and finds a waterfall. What had taken many people to read days, I did it in hours. I remember falling on my knees and thanking God, I felt His care.

Surprisingly, someone knocked on the door very strongly; I startled and ran to the door to see who it was. It was my brother with the youth group from church. My mom told him she was worried, and he came to bring me a word of encouragement along with worship songs.

After they left, I was filled with hope and peace, I rushed to get my children, and asked for forgiveness over and over. We enjoyed that evening together like we had not done it in a long time.

The book that "old lady" sold me had the information I needed and gave me the key to change my mood and way of thinking. The problems were the same, but I had changed my attitude towards them.

The book helped me understand that suicide was not an exit. This writer and professor from the University of Southern California was impacted by the suicide of one of his students, as a result of that, he developed a program to teach his students to live and love life.

The next day, I returned to the library, I looked for her to let her know how God had used her and infinitely thank her for her INSISTENCE. I did not see her, so I went to the counter and asked the employee for the lady who the day before sold me a book. I gave her a brief description and explained that she was dusting the books that were on the outside table with a "blue duster." The employee looked at me as if I was crazy and told me they did not have an employee with that description.

I insisted and asked for the duster, the employee with a terrible manner went and got the duster and showed it to me, and yes, it was in effect the "blue duster." I asked if the lady could be a volunteer or maybe the owner of the store or who knows if a client, but the young girl, upset by my insistence told me that that day she had worked all day at the store, and that no one had ever dusted the books. She recommended that I review my memory because maybe I had mistaken the library. I doubted briefly and asked if there was another library, and she said, "NO." Who was that sweet elderly, with a beautiful smile and capable of recognizing what my need was? How she sold me a book that was inspired by a suicide? I know God knows our limitations and looks for ways to place people or angels in our way to show us the exit when we cannot see it.

Statistics of 2012 in the United States shows that 10 in every 100,000 people take their lives. What can bring us to see suicide as an option or an exit? Not knowing how to face situations or problems, such as finances, personal, or passions; feeling abandoned by those we love; when we lose self-esteem and think we are worthless; when sickness arrives and we are not capable of facing it; when death snatches a loved one; when failure comes to our lives.

Thousands of reasons that can take us to see suicide as the door to freedom and rest. I thought it was my only option, but I was wrong. There could be thousands of reasons for suicide, but there are many more reasons to stay ALIVE. I feel privileged that God had put that angel in my path who showed me the way that pain and frustration did not let me see.

"Failure is not the end, but the beginning," with this thought, I ended the previous chapter, but it was not at this stage of my life I learned this concept. Many years passed before I comprehended it.

In my case, there was a combination of many situations that led me to think to the extreme. After having my daughter, the weight was a lot heavier. The attempts to keep moving forward did not give results. The financial, social, and emotional pressure and bad decisions had dragged me to chaos in all areas of my life.

Where was God? It was a question I asked daily. Today I understand He was always in the same place. When we feel guilty, sinful, and know we are not in order, we pull ourselves away and we don't have the courage to pray because we believe we are not worthy of His help. That was precisely my case, so I tried to solve things on my own.

I overcame the suicide, kept persevering and searching for an exit or maybe an entrance, towards what we call happiness.

One day, while I was working, I received a phone call. He identified himself as a young guy who was working in the summer program in offices of the company I was working for. It seemed brave from him to call me and let me know he found me pretty and interesting.

After that day, he continued calling day by day, insisting I went out for dinner with him. A young guy from summer? I mean, to me, he was a child. My co-workers made fun of me. A few times, I saw him in the hallway, and he was not really my type, so I tried avoiding his calls and would flee whenever I saw him at any place of the building.

One day after so much insistency, I accepted his invitation, but only so he would stop calling the office. I remember taking the kids to my mom's house so she could take care of them and I could go out with this young guy. Waiting for his arrival, I told my mom, "That guy does not leave me alone, he is not my type, besides he dresses like an old man, I am only going out so he can leave me alone." As I finished getting ready, my mom entered the room euphorically and said: "Girl, he just arrived, and that guy is HANDSOME." I said; "What? Mommy, please! You must have not seen him well because it is night-time. She insisted that I go out and not make him wait.

When I came out, I was BREATHLESS. He did not look at all like the guy from the company; he had blue jeans to his knees, with a white long sleeve's shirt. He had a tan and had spectacular legs, and the cologne he had on stayed in the entire house.

I tried to compose myself and not let him know how impressed I was. He was noticeably nervous and looked very timid. When we were on the way, I was the one asking the questions and he only responded with a strange tone of voice. It did not seem like his voice; it came out deep as an announcer inside a bath of echo.

After some time of having a conversation, I could not contain myself anymore and asked him if he had problems with his voice; he immediately cleared it up and started speaking normally. HILARIOUS! He knew there was a 10-year-old difference between us, so to impress me, he changed his tone of voice to sound more like a man.

After we were relaxed and talking with more trust, I did not doubt in asking him why he dressed "so serious" in the office, to not offend him, and say like an "old man," and smiling he said that he had just come from Texas. He started working and did not have office clothes, so his dad lent him his clothes. I said: "Well, you should change your "closet," and it would not be so hard to convince someone to go out with you." We laughed a lot and had a great night.

I would have never thought that night was the beginning of a relationship that marked the ending of a chapter and the beginning of another that completely transformed my life.

CHAPTER 10

Challenge

I DID NOT know how to start telling this part of my life. It was tough to choose a title for this chapter.

When I met this young guy, he was 18, and I was 28. It was a very noticeable difference. He was still in college and I had already graduated and was working for a few years. I was divorced and had two children. He was starting to live. Those were some of the "CONS" we had.

I obviously knew better than anyone else how hard a relationship with so much difference in age could be since I lived it with my own parents. My dad was older than my mom by 20 years.

I was vulnerable. I had been searching for that missing piece to complete me for years. Suddenly, one day, that someone who follows your steps appears, looking for any occasion to talk to you, to be close to you, looking for your admiration, your care and little by little wrapping you up in his environment you realize you like that feeling, it attracts you; and when you least imagine, you are trapped in a feeling you cannot control.

You can have all knowledge and experience in life, but no one can resist the impulse of love. It was late when I realized it, I was completely in love.

That was the easiest and simplest part of this story. Even if it seems impossible, it was not until I was completely in love, I discovered this young guy was the son of the vice president of the company I worked at. That was when things got complicated. What attitude can a mother have after caring for her son, and suddenly, she sees him falling in love with a divorced woman with two kids and 10 years older than him?

Exactly what you are thinking. That woman did not want to see me even if it was in paintings, and all with good reasons. We had to secretly see each other. To make things easier, I found a house and moved closer to where he lived.

After a short period of time and against all the advice and opinions I received, we decided to live together. In a way, I was happy; I felt that for the first time in a long time, someone accepted me as I was. Besides, he made an effort to adapt himself, accept my children, and all responsibility that represents.

The first few months were very hard, especially for him who was being bombarded by his family and friends who wanted to prevent him from making "the biggest mistake of his life."

Storms do not last forever. As the days passed, people got used to seeing us as a couple, including his mom.

It was incredible to see a young man of his age work tirelessly to help me get ahead. The part of the children was very hard, but as time passed both parts got used to it. With time, that imaginary line disappeared; to my children, he was dad, and for him, it was his children. It is not common to find that partner who feels genuine love and not feigned love for children who are not his own blood, in my case, it was even harder because it was someone younger than me. However, I was fortunate in that area.

In the beginning, the age difference did not affect us as a couple, but as time passed, when everything was calmed, and the "challenge" part passed, we became the typical couple. We had routine and divided responsibilities. Because of my type of job, he spent more with the children than with me.

When you get involved in this type of relationship, there are factors that will affect the relationship. Socially, we have different circles of friends. This brings insecurity to the couple. I was on a professional level, and he was just starting. At the beginning, these little things did not look harmful, with time, this provoked a chaos in the relationship.

Although I was older, he taught me a lot. He was a good administrator, and I always had problems in that area. Besides, he was very jealous of my children. He did not like leaving them under care; on the other hand, he had all the patience in the world to sit and study with my son. With him, I felt protected.

After two years together, we received the news that changed our lives; we were going to be parents. It is impossible to describe the joy we felt, especially him, since it would be his first blood son. It was nine months of preparation and celebration.

Almost to the due date, I received a call from my friend and brother, Dr. Velilla. He called to say hello and see how I was feeling, I expressed that I was perfectly fine, that the baby was very still and allowed me to sleep.

His intuition and experience made him suspect that something was not right, so he asked me to go see him. He immediately noticed that the baby was tangled in the umbilical cord, so I went to the hospital for an emergency, and after a few hours, I had my beautiful baby. I am infinitely grateful for Dr. Velilla's professionalism and experience, who saved the life of our baby.

The arrival of the baby completed our lives. The first few days, the father was like a lion protecting his cub. Those first few days were not easy because the overprotection for his firstborn provoked him to lose the objective of things. With time, he processed and adapted to his new role.

On the other side, our lives were much more complicated; we had more responsibilities in all aspects, especially financially. Besides, some situations arose that were giving me signals that he wanted to live experiences he omitted by committing to our relationship so young.

On some occasions and as many couples, we separated temporarily. I was unwilling to deal with his activities and adventures, and he just wanted to live what corresponded to his age.

His process to mature was long, tedious, and painful for me. But with time, everything started to get "normal." I knew he had many desires to surpass financially and was desperately searching how to make it.

The merger between the families happened. It was good and harmonious, especially with my mother in law, who became a very important part of our lives. She was our support, her help in those first years was vital.

In the same way, my family was also vital those first few years. My mother, as she always did, helped us in hard moments. I also remember that every Sunday, my father would come to visit and bring us groceries and spend hours playing with his grandchildren.

At this time, I had to live the strongest experience I have had to live; it marked the rest of my existence and that of my family.

Like in many countries, in Puerto Rico, we celebrate Father's Day. My siblings and I had the habit of visiting our father at the "grandparents" house (Rest in Peace). He lived at a home for adults/elderly; but every Father's Day, he waited for us at the grandparent's house.

It was not necessary to make a plan; he knew that, like every year, my siblings and I would go to pick him up. Then we would take him to the restaurant of his preference for lunch, where we would give him his gifts.

Unfortunately, that particular year, a situation was presented with my partner. Since I was so angry, I decided not to go to see my dad. I did not have the mood and was not going to be a good company. Besides, he would notice something was not right, and I did not want to worry my dad. I had peace knowing that my brother and sister would be there, and I was going the next day to bring him his gift and apologize.

The next day I was at my job and received a phone call, it was my aunt, my father's sister. She had never called me, so I thought the worst. She quickly clarified my dad was in good health, but she wanted to let me know that on "Father's Day," he waited for us all day and until dawn, and no one ever showed up. She said: "I saw him cry." You cannot imagine how those words broke my soul from pain.

For different life reasons, my brother and sister also had a complication and it was impossible for them to go. We all trusted that the others would be with our father. My dad did not have a phone, and with the rush of the day, we did not communicate. It seemed there was a perfect plan to ruin that Father's Day.

I immediately communicated with my brother and sister left our jobs and rushed to meet where he lived. We knocked on the door, and as he opened the door, we started to sing. He loved to hear us sing. As we sang, the doors of the neighbors and friends started to open, when he opened the door, we could see the excitement and pride in his eyes, because his friends and neighbors heard us singing. Then, energetic and surprised, he asked us what we were doing there when we were supposed to be working. We told him that our aunt called us and what he had said and almost in shouts, he said: "That aunt of yours is crazy, that is not true. I understand you guys had your reasons for not arriving. Besides, I do not know where she got that from. I cried."

We believed him, and that Monday, we celebrated Father's Day. It was beautiful to see how happy he was. We promised ourselves that it would never happen again.

Four months later, I received a call, our father was at the intensive care unit. He never told us that he suffered from the heart. He was 74 years old, and his heart was too big. The doctor asked to talk to us and let us know that he had been in treatment for a long time, but there was nothing else they could do, he did not have much longer to live.

That week was one of the hardest we had ever lived. I remember, on one occasion, I was visiting him alone at intensive care, and suddenly and desperately, he started asking me to leave the room. I did not want to and started calling the nurses. After a few minutes, I saw him going into a cardiac arrest, I began shouting until they pulled me out of the room. After some time and briefly recuperated, they let me in again. I will never forget his words: "You would avoid suffering if you learned to listen."

Saturday came, his favorite day, after the10 minutes of visitation in Intensive care, everyone went home. After a few hours, my brother came home to tell me that the time had come to run to the hospital because our father was agonizing.

Desperately, I arrived at the hospital. I do not remember how many people were reunited there, but the waiting room was filled with family, friend, brothers and sisters from the church. The pastor of the church immediately came to receive me and asked me to talk to my dad to give him peace so he could leave. I asked: "Why me? He could not answer, destroyed and with fear, I walked through that hallway until I got to the room where he was.

God! What an impression! He was surrounded by doctors and nurses and was breathing with difficulty, he seemed desperate. When he saw me, he took the oxygen mask off and asked them to leave us alone; he lacked air and could barely speak. He took a breath, drew strength, and firmly looking at me and, with authority, said to me: "Do not interrupt me, there is no time. Promise me you will not leave me waiting in heaven, like you did on FATHER'S DAY".

It is impossible to express in words what I felt at that moment. I was in denial, and only said: "You will be alright, nothing will happen to you." With his last breath, he shouted and demanded: "PROMISE ME!"

His pain and desperation confused me, as if I could not believe what he was asking from me. On the other hand, I knew that promise, even if it was the ONLY one, I had to keep it. Without time to analyze, I wanted to give him peace and to let him leave with the certainty that I would make an effort to keep what I promised.

I answer: "Yes, I promise". He immediately rested his head and looking up and avoiding looking at me said: "Now leave the room".

The pain had me paralyzed, confused, and nervous; I could barely give him a kiss and left just as he demanded. Minutes later, he left with the Lord.

Years had passed, and it still hurts as if I was living it right now. I have his desperate look recorded in my head. That promised that tormented me for years; why me? What could my father see at that moment?

CHAPTER 11

Beginning or end?

EVERYTHING SEEMED BACK to normal. We had a stable home. My partner achieved many of the goals he had set for himself, and he finally had his own business. Although we had situations, we managed, and I understand that our love was beating everything that, at some moment, affected us.

In the professional area, I had a new position and was financially well and pleased. I worked for a well-known company, and my co-workers were fabulous. We started the process of buying our dream home. How to forget the face of my children; everything was selected to their taste, I finally felt fully happy.

After a month of living in our house, one day, while working, I received a call that confused me. I could barely understand what my partner was telling me with a broken voice, he asked me to go down to the parking lot where a taxi was waiting for me. I refused to go without him giving me an explanation. He insisted that our lives were in danger and that I had to pick up the kids immediately and meet at a place the taxi already knew.

When I saw the seriousness of his call and desperation, I took my purse, ran to my great friend and supervisor's office, explained exactly what happened, and said goodbye thinking I would see him in a few days.

When I went down to the parking lot, the taxi was waiting. Thousands of thoughts ran through my head, I felt panic. As the cabbie was driving, he vainly tried to comfort me. Desperately, I asked God to take care of us.

We arrived at that shopping mall, within seconds, my partner appeared completely desperate and visibly worried. He gave me an envelope with cash money, and our boarding passes. He asked me to immediately pick up the kids and that he would find a way to communicate. He demanded me not to ask questions because he could not explain, just to trust him.

We said our goodbyes with pain and fear. The driver took me to pick up my kids, and I explained that we had to briefly go on an emergency trip. I felt my heart crumble when my oldest son asked me for the luggage. I tried to contain my desire to "shout" and cry, and I let him know that we did not need them because it was a short trip.

At that moment, I was not clear about the magnitude of the situation and was convinced that that nightmare was soon to pass, and everything would be back to normal.

My partner gave me precise instructions: "DO NOT CALL OR TALK TO ANYONE." Being at the airport and trying to contain myself so that the children would not get more nervous than they already were, I got desperate and wanted to warn my family. I called my mom and my sister, they had already been warned, so I briefly spoke and leaving my mother completely worried and desperate, I cut off the call. It was a hard and painful moment.

Ready to board, my body trembled, I had to contain myself because my children did not stop looking at me afraid, I did not allow them to detach from me for a second. We did not have luggage, and I did not know why or what was happening, but the sensation in my stomach and in my heart revealed the danger we were in.

Just before boarding the plane, I heard a voice from a distance calling me, when I looked back, my partner came running with his boarding pass in hand, we rushed to hug him, and we all cried together. We boarded without exchanging words. Once inside the airplane, he said: "I am sorry, but I cannot give you any details, you will have to trust me because the moment that I explain this to you, you become part of it.

Only my God knows what I felt at that moment, to see that airplane take off and look through that small window at everything I was leaving behind; my family, my friends, my job, my new home, my car, my entire life, and without knowing the reason.

I could see the desperation and pain in that man, but I was also able to see the love and desire to protect us. We landed in Florida, there was no going back. We had to start over and, overall, the responsibility to protect our children and move them forward, avoiding that this change affected them negatively.

Those first few months were hard; we had to simulate that everything was okay in front of the children. Everything was new for us, and adapting was difficult. That sensation felt in the stomach that you cannot explain. I felt that my life had no future, only a present that I was yet to comprehend.

When people listen to my experience, they always ask the same question: "Why did you not go back?" When you are in a situation like this, you cannot risk it and put in danger the life of those you love the most. You do not know who to trust or where to go. With time, I understood the dimension of the situation. It goes way beyond what I can write in this book for safety reasons, and above all because even if it affected our lives, that is not my story. It does not correspond to me to tell it.

It was a difficult transition. Thanks to the help of my uncles who lived in Florida, who without any fear gave us their hand, with time, we were able to rent a house, a car came after, and then I found a job. The only contact I was able to maintain, and with many measures, was with my mother and sister.

For months, they sent us a box here and there from Puerto Rico with the most important things. You had to see my children's faces every time they opened a box and saw some of their toys or a pair of shoes. It was very sad. It had been a while without knowing anything about my people on the island, something I tried blocking to not hurt myself more. I started visiting a church of my dad's denomination. There, we looked for God to remove the wounds and give us the peace we were yet to find.

Our decisions put us in difficult situations in life, and there is no way to stop the consequences. My husband had to go for a few years, and there was no way to stop it. A week before he left, he wanted us to get married.

Ironies of life! I did not plan anything this time, between my cousin and brothers and sisters from the church; they celebrated a simple and emotional wedding.

The day had come when I had to see my husband, already a man, leave. He had to serve with society. Life has changed us all, especially me. When I looked around me, I saw myself alone with three kids and a house to maintain. I could not show weakness, much less surrender, or say "I can't"; I had to keep moving forward because at that moment I was the only example they would have.

This has been the biggest challenge I've had in my life: my children. I knew that every decision I made would mark their lives forever. Their social and spiritual development would determine the success they had in life. I was wrong many times, made many mistakes, but I never gave them an example of defeat. I taught them to rejoice and be grateful in abundance and in need.

We had hard financial moments; we could barely get through. On the other hand, I could not stop supporting my husband and used to visit him weekly. For my youngest son, he was in the "Army." We were very jealous of the information we shared with him to not affect him, and that is how we maintained it for years.

My consecration with God went to another level; I learned to depend only on Him. Even if it seemed incredible, the government did NOT give me any assistance because I exceeded the income limit. How could that be possible? I earned a normal salary and had the expenses for three children, so almost every month, one of the services was suspended.

My situation was of desperation, I could not have contact with the people who would surely do anything to help me. And on the other hand, I could not show weakness or sadness to my kids; I had to pretend everything was good so they would not suffer; although it was hard for them not to notice.

I remember that a few times in winter, I had to wait for my co-workers to go homes while I waited in the parking lot. Once I confirmed that everyone left, I would run to the office and sleep because I did not have electricity, and we would freeze without a heater. There were many times that I went to sleep without eating because the food was not enough for me; many years that I never knew what it was to buy shoes or clothes. I lived out of charity and mercy from the brothers and sisters of the church or any angel that God crossed in our path.

There were many Christmases that my children received as presents. My credit had been affected by all the abrupt changes, which considerably affected our quality of life and our lifestyle.

My income was based on my job and the child support I received for my daughter. That was not enough to cover all the costs we had.

I never allowed my needs and circumstances to bring me to make incorrect decisions. Of course, I am not referring to paying with checks without funds or pawning things or borrowing money I was never able to pay back. All of that was in my life, I am referring to those "bits of help" that generally arrive and are given with something in "exchange."

I am a very humorous person, and besides everything, I never lost that part of my character. I was always a different mom. I looked for the fun side of things and always made my children smile or laugh. Always on our way to visit the "Army," we did it happily and enjoyed that "family" time. There was little time left for my husband to come back home, and that gave us encouragement and motivation to keep on fighting.

Despite the shortage, there was never missing in my children's education: GOD. I taught them to love and trust God, to believe that everything that seemed impossible, He could change it and transform it into something positive and real. I focused on teaching them that peace is not in the circumstances surrounding us, but in the trust, we have in God.

I remember that when they would wake up scared in the middle of the night wanting a light on, I would pray with them and teach them to see the light inside of them; then, I would turn off all the lights. That is how they learned not to fear and to completely trust their faith in God. Every time I got home from work, I would tell them a story or anecdote with an inspirational message or motivation to their lives.

Most of the time, they did NOT want to hear the stories because they preferred to play, but I would force them to sit down and pay attention. I knew that, eventually, they would remember when they grew up, just like it happened to me with everything my father had taught me.

I knew that, one day, they had to depend on their faith and not their circumstances; that was what sustained me until that moment. For three consecutive years, we assisted church every week and lived in complete order with God.

We were very content because, in a few months, everything was going to be like before, dad was coming back home. But one day everything changed, we arrived at the "Army" for the weekly visit and we were informed that my husband was no longer there.

I desperately looked for information, but they informed me that he had been transferred to another state due to a new accusation, and that they could not give me any more information. I was completely confused. What was very clear was that my husband would not come back home as we hoped for.

In my desperation, I decided to communicate with my people from the island, friends and family. I searched for information and everything I discovered was excruciating.

I had many mixed emotions. I realized, at that moment, the mistake I made accepting the relationship with that young man. I felt that I had put in him responsibilities and pressures that he was not prepared for yet. I realized the damage I had caused. Although with time I comprehended that it was not an excuse to not do things correctly.

From that moment, I communicated with the island. I contacted my family and the friends I left behind. This way, I discovered things that hurt me greatly. I felt rage and a pain that is impossible to describe in words. I left behind my entire life and had paid a very high price, and it was not until that moment that I knew the true motives.

My reaction was not adequate. I was filled with rage and blamed God for what was happening. I felt that God gave me His back. How could it be possible? I serve you, despite hunger and needs, I never stopped praising you. Because of love and gratitude, I did not go back to my island. I left behind my job, my friends, and remained faithful to the man I loved: "my husband."

I cried out to God: "I have always searched you: WHERE ARE YOU? What do I say to my kids now? I have taught them to trust in someone who apparently does not exist".

From that moment, I became a rebel towards God. The pain, the rage, and the frustration had taken over me. I forgot the promise I made to my father and started to doubt that a heaven truly existed. I never went back to church, nor did I want to pray.

The pain blinded me and made me forget about all the experiences I lived with God, and that showed me His love and how real he was.

As expected, away from God's guidance, I started making the worst decisions of my life, without caring who would be affected by them. I was never a person to go to clubs or drink, smoke, or use drugs. I never exposed my children to see me with men or gave them a bad example. My weakness was more emotional and spiritual, and it could be seen in my attitude towards life.

I let myself be dragged by my emotions and feelings, and by the desire to pull away from my life, everything that hurt me. Subtly and without planning it, I started a relationship that was completely wrong. I met adultery and the consequences of my bad decisions that affected both families.

These words sound very harsh, but there is no other way of saying it and I am not putting in this book a lie that avoids the purpose for which it was written.

Frankly, what I was doing hurt me, and thousands of times, we tried to break that relationship, but for the first time in many years, I did not feel alone. I was blinded, and it was impossible for me, at that moment, to realize the dimension of my mistake.

In the beginning, it was very hard, but with time, the storm passed, and it seemed like a normal relationship. My children got used to it, and there were good moments, others not so good. It was never a completely happy relationship. It was impossible. We cannot build happiness over another family's ruins and the misfortune of other people.

Back then, I was not conscious of the effects and consequences of that decision that would drastically change our lives. Many things changed, I had different friends and activities I was not used to. It was like living a life that did not belong to me.

This was the beginning…

CHAPTER 12

Running in the wrong direction

I USED TO go in the afternoons to a running track. I remember everyone running in direction to the right, including myself. It bothered me to see that this gentleman, very good looking, was always running to the opposite side. I thought he did it to get attention, and that would make me very upset. Inevitably, occasionally, our gazes would cross since we always found ourselves running the opposite way. One day after I finished running, I went to drink some water at the water fountain that was in the park. When I finished, he was there right behind me.

Without wasting any time, he asked: "Have we met?" ironically, I replied, "Of course we met. "He smiled and insisted, "Then, you know me?" I answered again with the same tone, "Who doesn't know you? You are the one who runs backward." Like a complete gentleman, he smiled, lowering his head, and after a few seconds, he said to me: "Have you ever asked yourself why everyone runs to the right? I don't see any sign that indicates it as a rule. Maybe I am the only one running the right way, and the rest are running the wrong way."

I was in complete silence, I felt dumb. He was right. By instinct, we are used to following along with the current, so we do not become the discordant note to not get attention.

From that day, he was not the only one running on the left side; I also started running on the left side and sometimes on the right. I decided, depending on which side I felt like running.

There are moments in life where we feel dragged by the currents. We make decisions that do not make us happy, and the consequences start to control what we think and do as if we were puppets of the circumstances.

I was not happy, I knew I had made a mistake; but it was too late to retract myself, I had to keep moving forward. My group of friends and everyone who surrounded me, at that moment, seemed to be covered with an invisible cloud that avoided me to see ahead while I was around them. I did not comprehend why those past few years, I was involved in situations, gossip, and things that kept me completely empty, but I was still persevering trying to understand what my destiny was.

The most important thing for me was my children. At that time, I lived a hard experience with my oldest son, who was 18 years old. I did not have the resources to give him everything he deserved; he learned to work and bought his first car. Then the girlfriend came, he seemed happy. Like any other guy at his age, he lived trying to discover his future and purpose.

One day he gave me the news that destroyed my heart. He got his girlfriend pregnant. I refused to accept it; I went crazy and spent five days crying.

My son confronted me and told me: "If you don't accept her and my baby, you don't accept me. You taught me to be responsible, and that's what I will do." I knew that my attitude could cause distance between us, so I surrendered. I helped them find their apartment, and after some time, already resigned, I started to fall in love with the idea of becoming a grandmother.

My granddaughter was born, it was an incredible and wonderful experience. We were grateful and celebrated that birth with joy. After weeks passed, all that joy became pain and frustration. Certain situations happened that I prefer not to detail out of respect for the parties involved. She had confirmed to my son that it was not his daughter and gave him a DNA test result as evidence.

I had never seen my son suffer so much. I saw him cry, shout, and question God. He became crazy, he was filled with resentment and was only thinking about revenge. After a few months, he did not look like the sweet and obedient child I had. He fell into drugs, stole, and got so many traffic citations that he ended up losing his license for five years.

My days had turned into complete hell. The concern did not let me sleep searching for options and trying not to lose sanity. I felt that at any moment, I would receive news that would destroy me.

One day the news arrived, he was in jail. I desperately rushed, looking for him, but it was not easy to have access to him anymore. I had to go through a tedious process to be able to get to him. When I saw him behind bars, then I turned to look at God.

It was impossible to keep refusing myself to talk to God. My distance and my separation led my family and me to destruction. I fell on my knees humbled, asking for forgiveness and promised that if He took my son out of there, I would serve Him forever.

The time my son spent in jail, I remained inside my car at the parking lot, crying out and shouting. When he was released, I knew I had to keep that promise. I ran to take him to a church where not too long ago, I met the pastor. It was a small church, but I was able to know the true power of God. In that place, there was no luxury or protocol. The people were the humblest ones I have ever met, but you could feel God's presence.

At first, my son felt uncomfortable, but after a few visits, he started to give his life to God. After a few months, he met a young girl. It was hard for her parents to accept him with the history he had, but with time it could be overcome. My son got married and was able to fulfill his dream to become a father with three beautiful children.

My son is a faithful and dedicated servant of God. Like me, he had to pay a high price for his ministry. God allowed him to live an even tougher experience than the first time, but his obedience, discipline, faith, and love for the Father, helped him keep moving forward. Today he has a testimony of victory, officially ordained as an evangelist, servant, and worker for the Kingdom of God. He inspires me, corrects me, orients me, and teaches me. His perseverance has taken him to another level with God.

God specializes in transforming the negative into positive, and this was not the exception. After seeing my son in jail, my life made a radical change. I was not willing to run in the same direction; everyone around me was running. I started to drift apart from friends who did not edify my life and made drastic changes. Although my partner did not understand the change, with time and my testimony, he started to accept it.

We started to do a business that bettered our finances considerably. He was working full time in the business. We determined that the most convenient thing was moving in together. We found a beautiful house, extremely spacious and in a very safe neighborhood.

After a month of moving in together, we received a phone call that froze our souls. Because of the economic crisis and other situations that happened, practically within a week, I had lost my business. There was no way of recuperating what we lost, so we remained in a deep silence, we both knew what that meant.

After a pause, he said that he had to move up north because we could not pay our expenses. At that precise moment, I felt it was the end of the relationship. We did not have a firm base. The relationship did not start correctly, it would not resist the pressure much less if they were economical. His departure was painful; with it, he took all his belongings. The house ended up completely empty. Being so spacious, we spoke and heard our echo; for me, it was a punishment arriving at that place that had turned into a nightmare.

I was only able to sustain myself for four months, until I had to accept the invitation of a great friend to move into her mobile home for a while, until I recovered. I couldn't maintain the expenses of that house.

My friend lived on a beautiful farm with barns and many animals. It was hard to accept in the beginning. It was a hard hit to my pride. But I did not have an option, so with pain, I surrendered my house and with her, the investment I had made; and in the small pick up my friend owned, moved the few things I had left.

This was not the first time I saw myself forced to start over. So, aside from the pain, I was feeling, I was grateful to God and my friend, who was an angel for us. Of this stay, we made an adventure; we looked for the fun side in the situation to avoid my children being affected by the drastic change we had made.

I often had to go running and hide in the barns to cry and release all that rage and frustration I felt. It was painful seeing my kids again without anything, but even with that, they never questioned me.

In just a few months, I lost my business, my house, my belongings, and the "love" that truly never belonged to me.

The decision I had made years ago out of impulse, revenge, or simply because of pain, where I sacrificed an entire family including mine, was never going to give me a happy ending. I felt that life was returning pain for my mistake.

My relationship with God was intimate, so I never questioned Him. I recognized those were the consequences of my mistake, and I only asked

Him to help me learn from that experience and give me the resources to get back up.

After a few months of living with my friend, I was able to save enough money to move into a beautiful apartment. My children's faces were priceless. I remember we did not set foot in that apartment until we dedicated it to God and recognized that He had done it for us.

This experience taught me so many things, and between those things, He showed me that we must be very careful with what we ask of God. I was not happy with the life I was living; when I reconciled with God, I said to Him: "I am not happy with my life; I need you to take it and do whatever it takes for me to be happy."

He did exactly what I asked Him to do. We cannot change our mistakes or the consequences, but we can improve our attitude. Everything is in our determination to change and do things differently.

God knows our limitations, and He knew that even if I had the desire, I was lacking willingness. So, at the moment, I gave Him the authorization, He did it.

When I was getting closer to this chapter, where I had to talk about the relationship of adultery, I knew it would be impossible to talk about it if I did not ask for forgiveness. Sometimes we feel that repentance and asking God for forgiveness is enough, but we are lying to ourselves, and it is a very irresponsible act from our part.

For years I debated with myself and repeatedly asked God to give me the strength to do what I knew I HAD TO DO. I woke up one day and decided; I picked up the phone and called the most affected person in the story. I humbled myself and, with a lot of pain, asked for forgiveness. I cannot change the harm I caused in them, but I made sure to let them know about my repentance and how hard life had made me pay for my mistake.

BEVERLY RUIZ

I never imagined that the lesson the man in the park had given me could be understood and applied many years later in my life.

By instinct, we will run and flow with the current, but that does not mean that we can change our path if we determine it with authority. Running against the current is the only way to obtain different results. My race had changed directions. This was the ending and the beginning of a new stage in my life.

CHAPTER 13

The promise

S O FAR, THINGS have not been easy for me. I spent too much time distracted in daily life situations. So distracted, that God managed to remind me that promise I made to my father.

My son continued with his license suspended, and his wife did not drive, so every morning, I would pick him up from work. That day, his wife wanted to come with me.

We arrived at his job, and as usual, we parked waiting for him, and suddenly everyone started to come out. My son came opening a way between the people, he seemed troubled. We thought he was fired. As soon as he entered the car, he asked us to leave quickly. I immediately asked him, "They fired you?" He said: "No, something incredible happened and I have to tell you guys." Already calmed, I looked to park in a quieter area.

He said: "Mom, I have a message for you." I was anxious, and I wanted him to show it to me immediately. Then he started telling us that he usually is by himself in his work area since it is a night shift, the only time he has company is when it is time for dinner when he gets together with all his coworkers.

That night was different. While a machine he was working with completed its process, he took a paper of purchase order and started to draw on the back of the page. His intention was to draw me. He took a few photos, and for some reason, he focused on the photo he had from his grandfather. He said he submerged himself into that drawing giving it details and shading.

He described that he felt a peace that he had never experimented with before. He had the sensation that someone was observing. When he finished his drawing, he was so surprised that he did not know how to react. He noticed it was time to leave work. How could it be possible for the time to pass by so fast? Besides, WHERE WERE HIS COWORKERS WHO ALWAYS LOOKED FOR HIM TO HAVE DINNER?

He called his coworkers, and they told him they fell asleep. Already desperate to know, I insisted on showing me the drawing. I remember that with his beautiful eyes filled with tears, he said: "Mom, I don't think you are ready for what you are about to see."

When he handed me the drawing, OH MY GOD! I felt I would dissipate; the impression was so big that I cried without consolation and, at the same time, laughed as if I had gone crazy. God managed the way to remind me I had a promise to fulfill.

My son drew my dad to PERFECTION. My father died when he was only 10 years of age. In the drawing, my father has a Bible and a message written with no spelling errors, a surprising fact since my son does not write Spanish well. The message said: "MY GIRL, YOU PROMISED ME, AND I TRUST IN YOU; DO NOT GIVE UP BECAUSE I WILL WAIT HERE FOR YOU."

Why did God want to remind me of that promise precisely at that moment of my life? The love of God surpasses all understanding. He knew that hard moments awaited me where it would be very easy to falter again. Many things happened after that divine message. I lived very hard moments and others of joy, but I knew it was still not time to understand the message God had sent me.

With time I had organized and was enjoying that new stage of my life. I felt pleased and comfortable. My children had taken different paths, but they were all heading in the right direction.

On my part, I was also at another level. I continued in my job for fourteen years. I became the leader of the worship group of my church and received the position of Director of Young Adults of District 10 in the east area of Florida at Council level. My first thought when I received that challenge was to say NO, but I understood that everything I had gone through in life was for training to perform with responsibility and authority in this position, so I accepted it.

I share this information, not with the intent of boasting, but to show you how a decision can transform our entire life. These last few years, I have had the opportunity to work as a counselor. There have been many experiences that have taken me to another level as a person and as a servant of God.

After reviewing all my family's success and mine, I must recognize that a part of me was still empty and needed to be filled with LOVE, where did I leave it? It was hard to rebuild my life again, even if there was a person who had become special, his circumstances did not allow him to formalize the relationship. I waited with the hope that someday all the barriers disappeared, but it never happened. Besides the frustration this provoked, I knew this relationship was not part of God's plan, and I had to keep going.

Although I never lacked options and offers from people who were willing to make me happy, being wrong so many times in the past, made me become selective and focus on the defects of the prospects and did not let myself be impressed by their virtues. I knew that if I could live with the defects, I would be ready to love again.

There is a moment in our lives that we think we lived it all. But life can surprise us at the moment we least expected. Age and maturity do not make us exempt from making faults and mistakes. We can be mature in some areas of our life and ignorant in others. I learned this lesson in a painful way. The experience was fundamental and helped me challenge my own strength.

For the last five years, I started traveling to Puerto Rico to celebrate my birthday with my family and childhood friends. One of the things that I enjoy the most is when my friends and I take our traditional yearly group photo.

Arriving on the island always fills me with happiness and energy that I cannot even explain myself. Within a few days, I wanted to go around the entire island, visit my family and my friends, go to every store, eat every traditional food and of course visit the beautiful beaches. I love going back to Florida with my skin tanned with the sun of my homeland.

On this occasion and after spending some days with my mom, I anxiously waited for the weekend to spend time with my friends. I remember that that Friday morning I went to the beach alone, a beautiful day! The beauty of my island is something that cannot be described with words. My skin was tanned in the sun and the smell of the ocean, and the breeze transported me out of this world.

After spending a nice day in full relaxation and peace, I returned to my sister's house, where I was staying. I found my mother supervising a man who was doing construction work on the house. When I parked, I noticed the worker looking at my car insistently. He seemed very handsome and interesting. I was a little nervous and rushed to get into the house as soon as possible to avoid being seen by him in the conditions I was, with my hair full of saltwater and sand.

Once inside, ready to take a shower, my mom started to knock on the door and insisted that I came out to introduce me to that gentleman who was a friend of my mom and sister. He had to leave and could not wait until I finished taking a shower, so I fixed myself as best as possible and went outside to meet him. I immediately apologized for my appearance and greeted him very educated.

After exchanging some brief words, he invited me out to a small farewell party they had for one of his friends who was leaving for the Army. He insisted that I accepted the invitation since I was going back to Florida and we would not have the opportunity to get to know each other.

Although his honesty surprised me, I thanked him for the invitation, but I apologized because it was impossible for me to go since I already had a compromise with my sister that night. He still gave me his number just in case I changed my mind.

We said goodbye, and my mother, very content, talked to me about the seriousness of that man. She told me everything she knew about him and suggested that I call him and not to waste the opportunity to get to know him better.

That night, as planned, I went out to meet with my sister. Our meeting ended earlier than I imagined, and I was left alone a Friday night. I did not want to go back to the house. I wanted to take advantage of every second on the island. I tried to contact my friends, but no one responded. Suddenly, I remembered the invitation of the construction worker to the party. I looked for his phone number, and although I doubted that I would call him, I preferred to call him and enjoy what was left of the night. Besides, what could I lose? He was known by my sister and my mom, and they appreciated him very much, so nothing could happen.

The cell phone rang barely twice, and he answered excitedly. He thanked me again and again for calling him. I felt honored by his reaction, and it seemed very nice of him. We coordinated to meet and have coffee and agreed that he would come to my location.

I waited a long time and started to get anxious until he finally called. He apologized for the delay and explained that he had gone to his house to change his clothes. At that moment, I was in San Juan, the capital of the island, and where transit is generally impossible on the weekends.

He suggested that I drove to his father's house since I would be driving against traffic. Otherwise, he would take too long to get to where I was.

I doubted going to his house, but the truth is that I waited for a long time. On the other side, what he was saying had logic, so I immediately started driving to his house. It was easy to locate his address since I grew up very close to that place.

I arrived at his house very nervous, and just like he said, he was waiting outside with his father. He was dressed casually; he looked very nice and very different from when I met him. He was a tall man, maybe 6'3", had a toned body and his cinnamon colored skin made a perfect match with the color of his eyes. The fact that he was a military man for over 20 years made me feel safe.

After introducing me to his father, he asked me which car I preferred to go, mine or his. I preferred it to be mine, it made me feel safer. I asked him to drive because many things had changed since I left the island, mainly the routes. He immediately took the wheel and suggested we go through a route that would take us faster to where we wanted to drink the coffee.

Throughout the way, we started talking about his experiences in the army, his family, and the reasons that led him to get a license to see his mother, who was sick. Unfortunately, she died, and he was temporarily accompanying his father while he signed again with the army. It seemed to me sweet of him.

Then it was time to talk to him a little about my life. After a few minutes of conversation, I realized he had diverted from the route and took another way that I also knew. I interrupted what I was telling him to ask why he diverted.

In a humorous way, he wanted to calm me down and insisted on continuing that route. I changed my attitude, felt uncomfortable; from his tone of voice, I perceived something was not right. I tried to maintain the calm and not exaggerate my concern; after all, he knew the way better than I did.

After a few minutes, he noticed I was tense. Intending to calm me down, he placed his hand on my thigh and said: "You already are an adult woman, do not behave like a girl, I am just looking for a place where we can talk quietly."

At that moment, I knew I was completely lost. Within seconds I reviewed everything that was against me: #1. I called his phone #2. I went to pick him up at his house #3. He got in my car, and I allowed him to drive #4. No one, except his father, knew where and with who I was.

I felt panic, but I knew I had to manage things with intelligence to not lose control since I ignored what type of person I was with.

We remained in silence for a few minutes. I was praying and begging God to take me out of the situation I put myself in.

I had hoped that he would take the route that would lead us to the place we decided to have coffee at some point. Unfortunately for me, he diverted and took the route that took us directly to a motel with a bad reputation in the area.

The distance between the intersection and the "motel" is extremely short, I did not have much time to act. So, I insisted and visibly desperate I demanded him to go back, he ignored my plea. At that point, I completely lost control. I only thought to jump out of the car,

I tried to unlock the door, but he locked it again without allowing me to achieve my objective.

He accelerated the car, and within seconds, we were at the entrance of the "motel," where a guy was in a golf cart directing people and charging the entrance. He only reduced speed, greeted him from afar with his hand and without paying, he entered one of the garages that were open.

Everything happened so fast that I did not have the time to make any signal. It seemed that everything was planned.

For the benefit of those who do not know this type of "motel," I'll explain, it is a place with small rooms with a private garage and they are rented for hours. There are some for sexual purposes and are equipped according to the customer's needs.

When I saw myself inside that garage, panic ran through my entire body, he took my cellular phone and got out of the car quickly. I knew it would be impossible to face him, on the other hand, I could not open the garage door by myself, he would have caught me before I was able to make it.

Thousands of thoughts ran through my head, the fear betrayed me. As I prayed, I thought about my children and my mom, in the immense pain they would suffer if something was to happen to me.

I stayed immobilized in my car; he knocked on the window and asked me to get out of the car. When I did not agree, he opened with the key and insisted that I calm down and get out of the car. I had no options; I got out and entered the room.

I knew that he had control at that moment, so using psychology, I calmed myself down and subtly insisted on going to another place since I did not like that one, making him think that I accepted the idea. I was ignored once again. It seemed as if he was not hearing. He immediately took off his clothes, threw himself on the bed with my cellular phone and my car keys under his pillow and said: "Now relax and tell me about your life." I was convinced that he was completely crazy.

I remained seated on the corner of the bed in silence. I kept praying, desperately asking God over and over to take me out of that place. I thought the worst, I thought that man would never let me leave that place alive. I imagined that after he satisfied his desire, he would kill me. Amongst my thoughts, prayers, and the panic, I do not remember exactly what he was talking to me about. The minutes I spent in that place felt eternal.

There was silence, and for a few seconds, I thought he fell asleep. He suddenly got up, grabbed me, and threw me on the bed saying: "Love, relax, and rest, I am not going to hurt you." His face was so close to mine that I could smell the strong scent of alcohol in his breath.

I tried to break free, and he made more force and said: "It will be easier if you relax, you'll see you will like it." A few seconds later, he ripped my clothes. I tried to resist, but he made support over my arms to make sure I could not escape. He had all his weight over my arms, leaving me completely immobilized.

Out of respect and consideration to my family, I will not be giving any more details of his abuse. After releasing his animal passion, he ended up lying on top of me without moving. I thought he was unconscious, but when I tried to move, he immediately woke up.

He hugged me after a few seconds and told me that I was the woman of his dreams and that he would never leave me. He got off me and made sure, once again, that my keys and my cellular phone were under the pillow and laid down, inviting me to lay down with him.

I was immobilized for a few minutes in complete silence, trying to convince myself that everything was a nightmare. I looked at everything

BEVERLY RUIZ

around me and the place I was in and could not believe what had happened to me. I could not cry at that moment; my mind was wandering off. I felt repulsed, disgusted; I looked at him again, and at that instant, I would have wanted to kill him, but how? I could barely move.

My body was in complete shock, and everything was trembling, but I knew that if I showed any symptoms of discomfort or disgust, he would get worried and hurt me to avoid getting accused. So, I did the best I could to walk to the bathroom and shower as he snoozed. Only God knows how I was feeling at that moment. I felt panic, thinking that he would wake up at any time and kill me.

After some time, my cell phone started ringing over and over. He saw that it was my niece; she was worried because I was not home yet. So, he asked me to answer the phone and tell her that I was on my way. At that moment, I felt a sense of relief.

As he drove back to his house, he talked to me about the plans he had for that night and his trip to visit me in Florida. I could clearly see that he had a mental problem, was drugged, or was cynic enough to not realize what he had done.

Once in his house, he said goodbye like a man in love. In a sarcastic way, he told me that I was not going to be free from him so easily. I performed the best act of my life, pretending that I was relaxed and smiling while listening to his plans.

When I was finally able to grab the steering wheel, I said goodbye and quickly left that place. Once far away from his house, I had to pull over on the side of the road and shout, cry and throw up. My body trembled uncontrollably.

I thought I would die from pain, rage, vulnerability, frustration, and fear. My entire life, I criticized women who were raped as an adult.

Ignorantly, I thought that a man goes as far as we allow. My entire life was transformed in those hours.

I thanked God for being alive. If that man had killed me, how would anyone know it was him? Thousands of thoughts crossed my mind. I did not know what to do. I thought that if I called the police and accused him, being a sergeant in the Army, he would surely change the story. I gave him all the necessary tools to sustain his version of events. Within seconds I imagined the magnitude of the problem I would be involved in.

I had a mix of emotions. The physical pain could not compare with the emotional pain and the frustration I felt, the impotence of not being able to defend myself. On the other side, I was afraid that I could have contracted a disease.

I got to my sister's house in silence, entered the bathroom to shower, and with the soap tried to erase the traces of that infernal night. I cried for long hours, but I had already decided that I was not going to say anything, if I was healthy. I decided to be checked by my doctor as soon as I landed in Florida.

That night was a photoshoot with my childhood friends. As hard as I tried to distract myself and have fun as I always did, my chest was tight and felt a lot of shame. I felt guilty and was afraid to say what had happened to me. I made the biggest effort to conceal the pain and the sadness I felt. I did not want to ruin that moment that was always so precious and unique for us.

I received many calls from that man, and I obviously never answered any of them. I came back to Florida and immediately went to see my doctor. I told him everything, and besides his insistence, I did not agree to press charges on the island. He performed all corresponding exams, I had to wait a few weeks, that became eternal, and thank God, all the results came back negative. I repeated all the tests every three months to confirm that everything was in order.

As time passed, I felt worse. I could not be at peace and felt that I had to do something more, so I called an ex-classmate and Captain of The Army. I asked for his discretion and told him what happened. He was hysterical and insisted that I pressed charges, he wanted to send him to prison, but I did not want to expose myself to that scandal. So, I asked my friend to verify his mental and physical record. Thank God the man was in perfect physical health, but mentally from what I had experienced, he was definitely not.

Again, and again, those memories consumed me. I was always a strong woman, and since I was a young girl, I had fought to not be sexually abused. How could it be possible that this happens to me already as an adult and with grandchildren? I reproached my ignorance and felt completely responsible and guilty.

After a few days, I was still feeling my chest tight, I did not have the desire to pray, and everyone knew that something was wrong with me. One of my best friends invited me to eat; he had noticed that I came from the island differently. That day, in the middle of the conversation, I was able to open my heart and tell him almost in "shouts" what had happened, and I said to him: "You know what? I have two options, this experience finishes me, depresses me, and I live the rest of my life regretting and feeling sorry for myself or I take advantage of it and use it as a step to keep going forward". Then I had already decided, I WILL WRITE A BOOK.

Since I was a little girl, it has been my dream and had never searched for the moment to work in it. I needed to spill over my life, remember, and bring out to light everything that had marked me positively and negatively. I knew there were chapters in my life that I never concluded; therefore, they were still present and hurting me.

That night I was able to free my soul. My friend heard me without interruption; practically in silence, he drove me back home. The next day, when I came home from work, I saw a big gift bag on my bed, when I opened it, it was a laptop with a beautiful card that invited me to make my dreams become a reality. My great friend had gifted me a laptop to start working on my dream.

It has not been easy to talk about this subject and relive that experience as I write it, but I know that my effort is not in vain. I will put in alert many women who like me, trust in their knowledge, experience, and maturity to detect danger. Misfortunes, abuse, and the mistreatments make no exception of age, sex, or experience. Any person, with all the experience of life, can suffer rape or abuse.

An experience becomes negative when we do not learn a lesson from it. This blow I received did not make me weaker, it made me stronger. I did not want to put my energy in revenge or hatred and be defeated by depression.

Heaven reminded me of the promise I made to my father. Now I can understand why He did it right in that moment of my life. God knew that my attitude towards this experience will put in play my salvation.

This experience motivated me to build my dream. On June 11, 2010, Friday at 12:00 pm, I sat down at the dining table with my laptop and started to write my book for the first time, "The Shout." The one you have in your hands today, the one that has been written with tears, laughter, and above all, with a lot of perseverance, love, and bravery.

I must confess that redacting this chapter, like many others, led me to relive each experience. I cried again, screamed, and felt pain, repudiation, and rage. But once I finished writing them, I was able to realize I had healed. The experience will be with me for the rest of my life, but they do not hurt me anymore, and they do not determine my present and much less my future. I comprehended that each experience made me an expert in the area and that, in the future, this testimony will serve to support all those men and women who had gone through a similar situation and have not been able to close that chapter in their lives.

I always had a dream, and this experience gave me the inspiration and strength to work on it, so even if what I will say sounds absurd, it was worth it.

"BUILDING OUR DREAMS CAN COST US TO FIGHT AND SUFFER A LIFETIME, BUT EVEN AT THAT IT IS WORTH TRYING"

CHAPTER 14

The shout of a deaf

REVIEWING MY LIFE and exposing it before all of you has not been easy, it has been a heroic act. I will probably be criticized in many ways. Some will be positive, and others will not be, but I am prepared to receive them with a humble heart and a positive attitude.

We all have a life, and we all can write a book about it. The intention of writing mine is to show you that the key of our success is learning to listen to the voice of God and to never stop fighting for our dreams; that we have to take what has hurt us and what we do not understand as a link that will help us climb up and reach our victory.

Besides the circumstances surrounding us from our childhood to our old age, God never stops talking to us. As I have proven throughout my life, He even "SHOUTS" if it is necessary if we listen to His voice.

When I started writing this book, I was in excessive tension. I was not feeling well, I felt dizzy, which made me nauseous; I felt so sick that I could not continue to write for a few weeks. Afraid of the way I was feeling and considering I had lost some hearing in the last few years, I decided to go to the doctor for a checkup.

He sent me to have an MRI done to check on my ear canal. After a few days, they called and asked me to stop by the doctor's office immediately. Once there, the doctor very subtly explained that my ear canal was perfect, I felt relief. However, the study detected that I suffered from a congenital disease called ARNOLD CHIARI SYNDROME, type 1.

"What is it?" I asked desperately. He looked for the simplest way to explain: "It is a malformation. It is a structural congenital defect in the base of the skull and cerebellum that affects the brain and the spinal cord." Obviously, at that moment, I did not understand absolutely anything he was talking about.

The part that impressed me the most was when he said that this malformation was classified as "rare." Only 1% of the population suffers from this condition. I do not know why I was surprised; usually, "rare" things happened to me, so it should not have been a surprise that I belonged to that 1%.

My next question was, "How long do I have to live?" I felt better when he smiled and said: "You have lived your entire life with it. I do not think you will die now, but you have to go see a neurologist as soon as possible, who specialized in your condition." He clarified that all the symptoms, including the loss of hearing, were due to the condition.

When I was already inside my car, I cried inconsolably; I thought, "God punished me". Within seconds, my mind went back and remembered that many years ago, I had suffered similar symptoms and reviewed that experience where I had pain.

For some reason, they called it "DRAMA," at the age of 13, when I least expected, I would lose consciousness and faint. By ignorance, they thought it was a pretended act to get attention. How could they think like that? Now that I think about it, I should have gone directly to a doctor to seek a professional opinion, but oh well, that is how it was managed back then. I remember it happened a few times.

One time, after I had left my house, it happened again. So, I decided to go to the doctor. They recommended going to see a specialist. I immediately went to see a neurologist, he only said I had excessive tension and sent me to therapy. I will not give the doctor's name, but I felt that he did not give the attention that I deserved. As I was explaining to him, he looked at me, skeptical. Probably seeing me so young and alone in his office made him doubt what I was explaining to him.

I do not remember exactly how, but my mother found out that I was sick. Back then, I only thought about hurting her, so with bad intentions, I let everyone know that they found a brain tumor in me. I can imagine the immense pain I put my parents through. I maintained the lie until they visited the doctor, and were very upset, he explained.

I will never forget when my father confronted me; his deformed face with pain and disappointment was more that I could bear. My rebellion and desire for vengeance crossed the line.

Today it is one of the few things that if I had the power to do so, I would CHANGE it. The pain that I caused in my parents for ignorance or vengeance was indescribable and unacceptable. Now that I am a mother, I could not bear to know that one of my kids had a brain tumor. It would devastate me; just thinking about it shakes my soul.

Now can you understand why, after I spoke to the doctor, I cried inconsolably and thought that God had punished me? Without knowing, I had declared to my parents, back then, something that was not far from the truth.

Losing hearing has not been easy. People get bothered when they must repeat what they said, and many times, I prefer to play dumb before asking: WHAT? I recognize that the lack of understanding hurts me. Even though I take everything in the best way possible, many times, the ironic mockery of some people bothers me.

When I came to the United States, it was difficult for me to learn the language. I have been mocked, but not always with bad intentions. So, I was relieved that, in a way, I had an excuse to justify my communication problem.

This condition helped me to go deeper in my message throughout this book. Although I am not completely deaf, I have difficulty hearing, and it is easier for me to get as close as I can to the person talking to me or raise the volume of the television, radio, or cellular phone to understand what they are saying.

We are like that spiritually as well. God has always talked to us, but our lack of faith, knowledge and sins separate us from him so much that the time comes where we cannot hear His voice. I was there many times, I got so far away from Him, that it was impossible to listen and understand what He wanted to say, I was twice as deaf.

I do not know if the probability that I end up completely deaf one day exists. It would be sad to not be able to hear the voice of my children, grandchildren, my partner, or the music that edifies me so much, but there is something I am sure of, I WILL NEVER STOP LISTENING TO THE VOICE OF GOD.

"I do not need my ear to hear you or my eyes to see you, I only need your presence inside me."

CHAPTER 15

My toolbox

REMEMBERING IS LIVING; many of those memories hurt, others make us laugh, and others simply makes us regret the opportunities we missed and that are never coming back.

Memories are a mirror of what your life was like. We must take the time and look in that mirror. You cannot change the past, but you will be able to work with those experiences in your present to have a better future.

When I started with this project, I had the obligation to remember. I realized that, like many people, there were memories that I simply blocked temporarily. I say temporarily because, at some point in our lives, we must bring them out again.

I removed my memories, then looked at myself in the mirror and realized that there were many things that I should have never done, and others that I never did. I was able to see how many dreams I stopped fulfilling, how many promises I broke, and what hurt the most was seeing the time I wasted fighting against the things I could not change or will never possess. Unfortunately, that time is not coming back. Is sad to recognize that if at that time, I had fought with the same strength for my dreams and enjoyed what really made me happy, I would have never met frustration.

I learned that God speaks. He uses all the resources and methods, giving us signs and sending angels to come out when we need them the most.

He also speaks through nature, music, parents, friends, and loneliness, but, even at that, we do not listen. Then, as a good father who loves his children, He "SHOUTS," to get our attention and force us to look at Him and listen to what He has to say. ***When all doors are closed, when we do not see an exit, and the only option is looking at God, that is what I call "The Shout of God."***

He spoke and "SHOUTED" at me throughout my entire life. His intention was to show me that nothing happens by coincidence; my experiences were my training ground. I did not understand and did not need to; I only had to believe, trust, and listen to what He had to say. His immense love and wisdom are sealed in each step we take, even when we make mistakes.

I am not saying that He uses sin to fulfill the purpose, but He allows situations in our lives, allowing us to make our own decisions. He lets us walk in the valley of shadow, death, and confusion so that we can develop our character and learn to depend on His grace and mercy.

He created the angels, amongst them "Lucifer." This was the best example given by the Father; It was impossible to appreciate heaven without hell. The pain is the strongest "shout" we can receive. When we experience the pain of death, betrayal, sickness, hunger, war and lies. When love vanishes or when we see injustice in life, such as children who are born sick, who without being able to start living, they are ready to die. When we see people getting drugged, killed and abusing children and elderly, while enjoying a healthy life. Meanwhile, there are brothers, sisters, and companions who work for the Kingdom of God waiting for a kidney or a heart to be able to continue serving God.

I can mention thousands of situations that cause us pain and frustration, but if that did not exist, we would never appreciate what we have. We would not know the mercy of God and would not be able to see the greatness of His power.

I always look for a homeless person who sleeps in the streets of the city I live in. He is very tall, and his skin is tanned, battered by the sun. He has long white hair, and his eyes are as blue as the sky. He is probabley around 60 years old, but the life he has had makes him look 80. For some inexplicable reason, I always think of him and look for him to give him money. On holidays, I bring him food and money, making sure that he is well during those festive days.

For two consecutive years, I tried without success, to talk to him, but his lost and firm stare was a clear sign that his mind was far away from what I was saying. I was driving one day by the area where he always had his things. I saw that his belongings were on the same bench as usual; some blankets and plastic bags, but he was not there that day. I got worried because he never left his things alone. When I focused, I saw him sitting down on the sidewalk, and with a stick, was pulling out the sand that accumulated in the small cracks.

I was on the opposite side of the street, so I had to make an abrupt turn. I parked, took some money with me, and walked towards him as fast as I could. I squatted down to his level and said to him: "Hi, how are you?" I thought that as always, he would not respond, but surprisingly he raised his head, looked at me, and smiling at me responded that he was well. I asked him if he was hungry and he said no, that he was good.

I tried to look for conversation and take advantage of that unique moment. I told him: "Do you know there are many people that care for you?" He said: "Yes, I know," as he continued to play with the stick. I continued telling him: "We pray and wish you to be well, but there is someone special that always looks out for you, protects you, and loves you very much, do you know who it is?" He stopped as if he was waiting for me to give him the answer to my question, so I continued saying: "His name is GOD!" He raised his head and, after a few seconds of silence and with a smile that allowed me to see all his damaged teeth, lifted his hands and pointing to heaven he said: "OF COURSE, WHO DO YOU THINK GAVE ME ALL THIS?"

I cannot describe in this paper everything that went through my mind in those couple of seconds. I looked at his dirty and ripped clothes, the bench where he had his only belongings, and then looked at myself. I realized that between him and me, I was the beggar.

I put the money in his hands and ran to my car. Without being able to drive, I started to cry, "SHOUT," and said: "God, forgive me for not realizing all the blessings you have given me. Forgive me for not being grateful, because You had to leave him without a house, clothes, and food, so I could see how blessed I am."

At that moment, I was "shouting" inside my car, but God had "shouted" at me first. He had shown me that happiness is not based in our possessions; that those who are not capable of recognizing the signs and blessings of heaven and are not listening to God's voice are the true beggars of life.

God created you. He made you special and unique. He predicted and predestined your life so that you can be an example to others. If you are going through difficulties, if you are in pain, then you are privileged. God is using you; He is putting you through fire just like the gold, to be refined.

Everything in life requires effort, there is no victory if you have not fought a battle. Even Jesus had to suffer and fight to return to heaven. If He, being the Son of God, had to battle to return to His home, what makes you think that you can make it without a fight? These wise words were said to me by my son Jonathan, and I will never forget them.

Gratitude, love, listening to God's voice, and being obedient are the keys to success. He will always give you signs. I have a great friend and pastor, Joivan Jiménez. In the first preaching I heard from him, he used an illustration that transformed my life and that I will never be able to forget. He spoke that, in order to define your dreams, you must learn to understand the signs. He said that Jesus was the perfect example; his carnal father, Joseph, was a carpenter. Use your imagination; look at Jesus as a child playing with wood, hammer, and nails. These were the signs that showed him his destiny and purpose on earth.

What are the signs that life has given you? What has God shown you? What have you had to live?

These were the same questions I asked myself. Searching for the answers, I ran to the mirror of memories and reviewed my life. I understood that God had given me the tools to build my dream. Every pain and experience I went through were my wood, hammer, and nails.

Jesus was nailed to the cross; it was the biggest act of love and victory. He resurrected on the third day and went back home. That way, he demonstrated the path we need to follow to obtain the victory. You must live the life corresponding to you, fight to obtain the victory, and then you will be able to enjoy your true home.

This book came into your hands as a "Shout" of alert to your life; run and look at yourself in the mirror. Review your life and find which are the signs that God has given you to build your dreams. To think and desire your dreams is not enough; you must fight for them.

Take your life and transform it into your toolbox; include love, faith, hope, gratitude, humility, will, and bravery in it to fight. God will be the Director of your work, listen to His voice whenever He speaks or "shout" at you trust and believe in His promises, start using your toolbox, and you will be able to see your dreams come true.

God is not responsible for building your dreams. He deposits in your heart the desire and the dream; He gave your life and experiences to use them as tools. Your job is to build it.

The work of your life depends only on you. Today is the perfect day to start building your dreams.

Note: This chapter was the first one to be written on June 11, 2010. Inspired by God, I wrote the final message of this book before writing anything else. I never came back to make changes or alter what I had written. Only a line was added to describe what "The Shout of God" is. I jealously kept this original, and He was my inspiration to write all the other fourteen chapters.

CREDITS

Translator:

Karla Franco

Editor:

Solimar García Hance

Reviwed:

Beverly Ann Faustinelli

Cover Designers:

Pedro Guadalupe Graphic designer
www.pedroguadalupe.com
email: pedroguadalupe@gmail.com
(787) 354-8887

Website designer:

Wilfred J. Lugo
Email: wilfredjlugo@gmail.com
(787) 515-5859

Design, art, and promotion:

Marlene Ruiz / Touch Creative Design
Email: ruizmarlene421@hotmail.com
(787) 595-7596

Images:

Josean A Espinosa/ photographer/
Luis Santos/ photographer

For personal presentations:

Email: ruizruizbeverly@gmail.com
Http:// www.beverlyruiz.com

Facebook & Instagram:

Beverly Ruiz / El Grito
(352) 804-5100
(787) 207-1144

BIOGRAPHY

Beverly Ruiz

B ORN MAY 20, 1963, in the city of Brooklyn, NY. Married and mother of three children and grandmother of six grandchildren.

Currently, Ruiz studies Business Administration and works as a writer, speaker, lecturer, and actress.

She began her career as an author in June 2010. She wrote her first book, "El Grito," a christian motivational autobiography. Her experiences and life events have been inspiring and an example of improvement for thousands of people.

As a result of its sales success, in January 2014, it began to make itself known through the press, social networks, radio, television programs, and personal presentations, reaching the sympathy and favorable acceptance of its public.

Sometime later, she began to work with different organizations that support abused and mistreated women. This exhibition leads her to become a Chaplain of the Government of Puerto Rico, speaker, and lecturer. In addition, she was appointed by the Department of Health of the municipality of the indigenous town of Ponce on the island of Puerto Rico as the godmother of "Almas Guerreras," an organization dedicated to offering support to abused women. This organization includes 17 Municipalities adjacent to the town of Ponce.

In 2015, she wrote the first screenplay for the play "Despeinada, Entre Risas y Vivencias," which was performed successfully at the Alejandro Tapia Theater in Old San Juan in Puerto Rico.

The play was later presented in the United States and managed to grab the press and media attention as it was the first Latino play to be presented at the Reilly Art Center in Ocala, FL, and at the Miller Center of the Arts in PA.

The author is currently presenting her new book *Madness with Sense* that is born inspired and a balm for humanity's soul amid the coronavirus pandemic.

Printed in the United States
By Bookmasters